# Software Best Practice 3

## ESSI Practitioners' Reports

**Springer**
Berlin
Heidelberg
New York
Barcelona
Hong Kong
London
Milan
Paris
Tokyo

Michael Haug   Eric W. Olsen
Gilles Vallet   Olivier Bécart (Eds.)

# Software Management Approaches: Project Management, Estimation, and Life Cycle Support

Software Best Practice 3

With 30 Figures and 14 Tables

Springer

*Editors:*

Michael Haug
Eric W. Olsen
HIGHWARE GmbH
Winzererstraße 46
80797 München, Germany

Michael@Haug.com
ewo@home.com

Gilles Vallet
Olivier Bécart
Editions HIGHWARE s.a.r.l.
43, rue Richer
75009 Paris, France

Gilles_Vallet@compuserve.com
olivier.becart@highware.fr

ISBN 3-540-41786-9 Springer-Verlag Berlin Heidelberg New York

Library of Congress Cataloging-in-Publication Data
Software best practice.
    p. cm.
    Includes bibliographical references and index.
    1. Software quality approaches : testing, verification, and validation / M. Haug,
E. W. Olsen, L. Consolini, eds. -- 2. Managing the change : software configuration and
change management / M. Haug ... [et al.], eds. -- 3. Software management approaches :
project management, estimation, and life cycle support / M. Haug ... [et al.], eds. --
4. Software process improvement : metrics, measurement, and process modelling /
M. Haug, E. W. Olsen, L. Bergman, eds.
    ISBN 3540417842 (v. 1) -- ISBN 3540417850 (v. 2) -- ISBN 3540417869 (v. 3) --
ISBN 3540417877 (v. 4)
    1. Software engineering. I. Haug, Michael, 1951-

QA76.758 .S6445 2001
005.1--dc21                                                         2001041181

Springer-Verlag Berlin Heidelberg New York,
a member of BertelsmannSpringer Science + Business Media GmbH

http://www.springer.de

© Springer-Verlag Berlin Heidelberg 2001
Printed in Germany

Cover design: design & production GmbH, Heidelberg
Typesetting: Camera-ready by editors
Printed on acid-free paper      SPIN: 10832687      45/3142 GF – 543210

# Foreword

C. Amting
Directorate General Information Society, European Commission, Brussels

Under the 4th Framework of European Research, the European Systems and Software Initiative (ESSI) was part of the ESPRIT Programme. This initiative funded more than 470 projects in the area of software and system process improvements. The majority of these projects were process improvement experiments carrying out and taking up new development processes, methods and technology within the software development process of a company. In addition, nodes (centres of expertise), European networks (organisations managing local activities), training and dissemination actions complemented the process improvement experiments.

ESSI aimed at improving the software development capabilities of European enterprises. It focused on best practice and helped European companies to develop world class skills and associated technologies to build the increasingly complex and varied systems needed to compete in the marketplace.

The dissemination activities were designed to build a forum, at European level, to exchange information and knowledge gained within process improvement experiments. Their major objective was to spread the message and the results of experiments to a wider audience, through a variety of different channels.

The European Experience Exchange (EUREX) project has been one of these dissemination activities within the European Systems and Software Initiative. EUREX has collected the results of practitioner reports from numerous workshops in Europe and presents, in this series of books, the results of Best Practice achievements in European Companies over the last few years.

EUREX assessed, classified and categorised the outcome of process improvement experiments. The theme based books will present the results of the particular problem areas. These reports are designed to help other companies facing software process improvement problems.

The results of the various projects collected in these books should encourage many companies facing similar problems to start some improvements on their own. Within the Information Society Technology (IST) programme under the 5th Framework of European Research, new take up and best practices activities will be launched in various Key Actions to encourage the companies in improving their business areas.

# Preface

M. Haug
HIGHWARE, Munich

In 1993, I was invited by Rainer Zimmermann and David Talbot to participate in the industrial consultation group for the then-new ESSI initiative. Coming from a Software Engineering background and having been responsible for industrial software production for more than 20 years, I was fascinated by the idea of tackling the ubiquitous software quality problem in a fresh new way, in helping not only a particular organisation to improve their software process, but to create the framework for an exchange of the experience gained among those organisations and beyond, to spread this experience throughout the European Software Industry.

While serving as an evaluator and reviewer to the Commission within the ESSI initiative, I had the opportunity to have a more or less superficial look at more than 100 Process Improvement Experiments (PIEs) at workshops, conferences and reviews. Consequently, the desire to collect and consolidate information about and experience from *all* of the more than 300 PIEs in a more organised way became immanent. In short, the idea for EUREX was born.

EUREX is an ESSI dissemination project. The budget limitations applicable to such projects did not allow us to conduct reviews or interviews of all of the more than 300 projects. Therefore, a distributed and staged approach was taken: a set of regional workshops became the platform to collect the information. The results of these 18 workshops held in Europe over a period of two years, together with contributions from representative PIEs and with expert articles rounding out the experience reports, is now in your hands: a series of books focussing on the central problem domains of Software Process Improvement.

Each of the books concentrates on a technical problem domain within the software engineering process, e.g. software testing, verification and quality management in Vol. 1. All of the books have a common structure:

Part I SPI, ESSI, EUREX describes the context of the European Software and Systems Initiative and the EUREX project. While Part I is similar in all books, the problem domains are differentiated for the reader. It consists of the chapters:

1 Software Process Improvement

2 The EUREX project

3 The EUREX taxonomy.

In Part II we present the collected findings and experiences of the process improvement experiments that dealt with issues related to the problem domain addressed by the book. Part II consists of the chapters:

4 Perspectives

5 Resources for Practitioners

6 Experience Reports

7 Lessons from the EUREX Workshops

8 Significant Results

Part III offers summary information for all the experiments that fall into the problem domain. These summaries, collected from publicly available sources, provide the reader with a wealth of information about each of the large number of projects undertaken. Part III includes the chapters:

9 Table of PIEs

10 Summaries of Process Improvement Experiment Reports

A book editor managed each of the books, compiling the contributions and writing the connecting chapters and paragraphs. Much of the material originates in papers written by the PIE organisations for presentation at EUREX workshops or for public documentation like the Final Reports. Whenever an author could be identified, we attribute the contributions to him or her. If it was not possible to identify a specific author, the source of the information is provided. If a chapter is without explicit reference to an author or a source, the book editor wrote it.

Many people contributed to EUREX[P1], more than I can express my appreciation to in such a short notice. Representative for all of them, my special thanks go to the following teams: David Talbot and Rainer Zimmermann (CEC) who made the ESSI initiative happen; Mechthild Rohen, Brian Holmes, Corinna Amting and Knud Lonsted, our Project Officers within the CEC, who accompanied the project patiently and gave valuable advice; Luisa Consolini and Elisabetta Papini, the Italian EUREX team, Manu de Uriarte, Jon Gómez and Iñaki Gómez, the Spanish EUREX team, Gilles Vallet and Olivier Bécart, the French EUREX team, Lars Bergman and Terttu Orci, the Nordic EUREX team and Wilhelm Braunschober, Bernhard Kölmel and Jörn Eisenbiegler, the German EUREX team; Eric W. Olsen has patiently reviewed numerous versions of all contributions; Carola, Sebastian and Julian have spent several hundred hours on shaping the various contributions into a consistent presentation. Last but certainly not least, Ingeborg Mayer and Hans Wössner continuously supported our efforts with their professional publishing know-how; Gabriele Fischer and Ulrike Drechsler patiently reviewed the many versions of the typoscripts.

The biggest reward for all of us will be, if you – the reader – find something in these pages useful to you and your organisation, or, even better, if we motivate you to implement Software Process Improvement within your organisation.

---

[P1] Opinions in these books are expressed solely on the behalf of the authors. The European Commission accepts no responsibility or liability whatsoever for the content.

# Table of Contents

# List of Contributors

Olivier Bécart
Editions HIGHWARE
olivier.becart@highware.fr

Adrian Cowderoy
Multimedia House of Quality
Adrian.Cowderoy@mmhq.co.uk

Eric W. Olsen
HIGHWARE
ewo@home.com

Fred Schindler
Philotech
Fred.Schindler@Philotech.de

Brian Chatters
ICL
bchatters@fjicl.com

Michael Haug
HIGHWARE
Michael_Haug@compuserve.com

Arnold Rochfeld
Rochfeld Consultants
Arnold.Rochfeld@wanadoo.fr

Gilles Vallet
Editions HIGHWARE
Gilles.Vallet@highware.fr

# Part I

## SPI, ESSI, EUREX

# 1 Software Process Improvement
# A European View

## 1.1 Introduction[1]

Enterprises in all developed sectors of the economy – not just the IT sector – are increasingly dependent on quality software-based IT systems. Such systems support management, production, and service functions in diverse organisations. Furthermore, the products and services now offered by the non-IT sectors, e.g., the automotive industry or the consumer electronics industry, increasingly contain a component of sophisticated software. For example, televisions require in excess of half a Megabyte of software code to provide the wide variety of functions we have come to expect from a domestic appliance. Similarly, the planning and execution of a cutting pattern in the garment industry is accomplished under software control, as are many safety-critical functions in the control of, e.g., aeroplanes, elevators, trains, and electricity generating plants. Today, approximately 70% of all software developed in Europe is developed in the non-IT sectors of the economy. This makes software a technological topic of considerable significance. As the information age develops, software will become even more pervasive and transparent. Consequently, the ability to produce software efficiently, effectively, and with consistently high quality will become increasingly important for all industries across Europe if they are to maintain and enhance their competitiveness.

## 1.2 Objectives – Scope of the Initiative

The goal of the European Systems and Software Initiative (ESSI) was to promote improvements in the software development process in industry, through the take-up of well-founded and established – but insufficiently deployed – methods and technologies, so as to achieve greater efficiency, higher quality, and greater economy. In short, the adoption of Software Best Practice.

---

[1] All material presented in Chapter 1 was taken from publicly available information issued by the European Commission in the course of the European Systems and Software Initiative (ESSI). It was compiled by the main editor to provide an overview of this programme.

The aim of the initiative was to ensure that European software developers in both user and vendor organisations continue to have the world class skills, the associated technology, and the improved practices necessary to build the increasingly complex and varied systems demanded by the market place. The full impact of the initiative for Europe will be achieved through a multiplier effect, with the dissemination of results across national borders and across industrial sectors.

## 1.3   Strategy

To achieve the above objectives, actions have been supported to:

- Raise awareness of the importance of the software development process to the competitiveness of all European industry.
- Demonstrate what can be done to improve software development practices through experimentation.
- Create communities of interest in Europe working to a common goal of improving software development practices.
- Raise the skill levels of software development professionals in Europe.

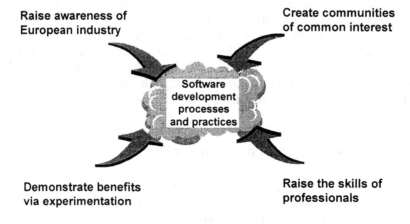

Fig. 1.1  A focused strategy for achieving Best Practice

## 1.4 Target Audience
## (Who can participate, Who will benefit)

Any organisation in any sector of the economy, which regards generation of software to be part of its operation, may benefit from the adoption of Software Best Practice. Such a user organisation is often not necessarily classified as being in the software industry, but may well be an engineering or commercial organisation in which the generation of software has emerged as a significant component of its operation. Indeed as the majority of software is produced by organisations in the non-IT sector and by small and medium sized enterprises (SMEs), it is these two groups who are likely to benefit the most from this initiative.

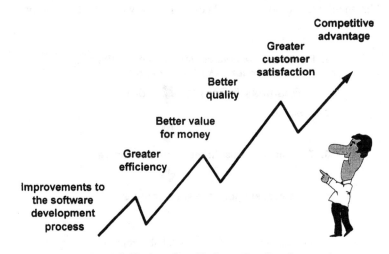

**Fig. 1.2** The benefits of Software Best Practice

In addition to the user organisations participating directly in the initiative, software vendors and service providers also stand to benefit, as demand for their methodologies, tools and services is stimulated and valuable feedback is given on the strengths and weaknesses of their offerings.

## 1.5 Dimensions of Software Best Practice

Software Best Practice activities focus on the continuous and stepwise improvement of software development processes and practices. Software process improvement should not be seen as a goal in itself but must be clearly linked to the business goals of an organisation. Software process improvement starts with addressing the organisational issues. Experiences in the past have shown that before any investments are made in true technology upgrades (through products like tools and infrastructure computer support) some critical process issues need to be addressed and solved. They concern how software is actually developed: the methodology and methods, and, especially, the organisation of the process of development and maintenance of software.

Organisational issues are more important than methods and improving methods is, in turn, more important than introducing the techniques and tools to support them.

Finding the right organisational framework, the right process model, the right methodology, the right supporting methods and techniques and the right mix of skills for a development team is a difficult matter and a long-term goal of any process improvement activity. Nevertheless, it is a fundamental requirement for the establishment of a well-defined and controlled software development process.

**1. Business:** *market, customers, competition, ...*
**& People issues:** *skills, culture, teamwork, ...*

**Business & People ↓ driven**

**2. Process**

↓

**3. Technical approach:** *methods, procedures, ...*

↓

**4. Technical support:** *tools, computers, ...*

**Fig. 1.3** Anatomy of a successful SPI programme

Software development is a people process and due consideration should be given to all the players involved. Process improvement and implementation concerns people and needs to take into account all people related aspects (human factors). These are orthogonal to the technology and methodology driven approaches and are crucial to the success of adopting best practice.

Successful management of change includes staff motivation, skilling and promotion of the positive contributions that staff can make.

The people aspects cover all the different groups which have an input to the software development process including Management, and Software Engineers.

In order to ensure an appropriate environment for the successful adherence to a total quality approach it is imperative that Senior Management are fully aware of all the issues. Their commitment and involvement are crucial to the successful implementation of the improvement process and it might be necessary to raise their awareness regarding this issue.

It is important to identify clear milestones that will enable the software developer to measure progress along the road of software improvement. Certification through schemes such as ISO 9000, while not an end in itself, can play a valuable role in marking and recognising this progress.

## 1.6   European Dimension

The objectives of Software Best Practice can be accomplished by understanding and applying the state-of-the-art in software engineering, in a wide range of industries and other sectors of the economy, taking into account moving targets and changing cultures in this rapidly evolving area. The full impact for Europe will then be achieved by a multiplier effect, with the dissemination of results across national borders and across industrial sectors.

The definition of best practice at the European level has three main advantages. Firstly, there is the matter of scale. Operating on a European-wide basis offers the possibility to harness the full range of software development experience that has been built up across the full spectrum of industry sectors in addition to offering exposure to the widest selection of specialist method and tool vendors. In the second place, it maximises the possibility to reduce duplication of effort. Finally, it offers the best possibility to reduce the present fragmentation of approaches and, at the same time, to provide a more coherent and homogeneous market for well-founded methods and tools.

Moreover, as we move towards the Information Society, we need to develop and build the technologies necessary to create the Information Infrastructure (such as is envisaged in the Commission White Paper on "Growth, Competitiveness and Employment"); a dynamic infrastructure of underlying technologies and services to facilitate fast and efficient access to information, according to continually changing requirements. Within this context, software is seen as a major enabling technology and the way in which we develop software is becoming a key factor for industrial competitiveness and prosperity.

All of the above factors can be enhanced through the creation and use of standards, including de-facto standards for "best practice" and, indeed, standards are vital in the long term. However, the proposed actions should not, at this stage of evolving standards, be restricted to one particular standard. Furthermore, the actions cannot wait for a full and accepted set to be established before being able to implement improvement. Nevertheless, a close look at the ISO-SPICE initiative and active contribution to it is suggested.

## 1.7   Types of Projects

The European Commission issued three Calls for Proposals for Software Best Practice in the Fourth Framework Programme in the years 1993, 1995 and 1996. The first call was referred to as the "ESSI Pilot Phase". The aim was to test the perceived relevance of the programme to its intended audience and the effectiveness of the implementation mechanisms. Before the second call in 1995 a major review and redirection took place. Following the revision of the ESPRIT Work programme in 1997, a further call was issued of which the results are not been reviewed in this book. The four calls varied slightly in their focus. In the following, all types of projects supported by the ESSI initiative will be presented.

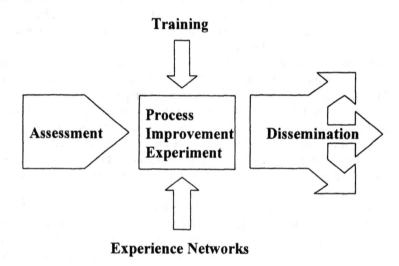

**Fig. 1.4** Lines of complementary action

### 1.7.1   Stand Alone Assessments[2]

The main objective of the Stand Alone Assessments action was to raise the awareness of user organisations to the possibilities for improvement in their software development process, as well as give the momentum for initiating the improvement process. Assessments were targeted particularly at organisations at the lower levels of software development maturity.

---

[2] Stand Alone Assessments have been called only in the year 1995.

It was expected that assessments will stimulate the pursuit of quality through continuous improvement of the software development process.

An underlying methodology was needed to carry out an assessment. This methodology had to recognise that software development is governed by the processes which an organisation uses to capitalise upon the potential talent of its employees (people) in order to produce competitive, top quality, software systems and services (products).

Most assessment methods are based on questionnaires and personnel interviews. An assessment resulted in the identification of an organisation's strengths and weaknesses, provides a comparison with the rest of the industry, and was accompanied by a series of recommendations on how to address the weak aspects of the software development process, from a technological and organisational point of view.

No single standard methodology was advocated; however, the adopted approach had to be a recognised assessment methodology, such as BOOTSTRAP, TickIT, etc.

The following types of assessment have been envisaged:

Self-assessments, which were conducted if the organisation had the required resource capacity to allow it to absorb the load of conducting the assessment. In this case, it was expected that an internal assessment team was set up, trained in the selected methodology, and that it carried out the assessment according to an agreed schedule. This type of assessment may have conducted with the support of the methodology provider or under the guidance of external assessors.

Assessments carried out by external assessors. The organisation was expected to select an external assessor who conducted the assessment. Again, an internal assessment team was expected to be set up to collaborate with the assessors.

Both types of assessment had to cater for measuring the organisation's existing situation, positioning the organisation relatively to the rest of the industry in terms of software development process and allowing the organisation to plan and prioritise for future improvements.

## 1.7.2 Process Improvement Experiments (PIEs)[3]

PIEs are aimed at demonstrating software process improvement. These followed a generic model and demonstrated the effectiveness of software process improvement experiments on an underlying baseline project that is tackling a real development need for the proposing organisation.

---

[3] Process Improvement Experiments have been called in the years 1995, 1996 and 1997. As the project type "Application Experiment" can be considered the predecessor of PIEs, it is legitimate to say that PIEs have been subject to all ESSI calls and have formed not only the bulk of projects but also the "heart" of the initiative.

Process Improvement Experiments (PIEs) formed the bulk of the Software Best Practice initiative. Their aim was to demonstrate the benefits of software process improvement through user experimentation. The results had to be disseminated both internally within the user organisations to improve software production and externally to the wider community to stimulate adoption of process improvement at a European level.

The emphasis was on continuous improvement through small, stepped actions. During a PIE, a user organisation undertook a controlled, limited experiment in process improvement, based on an underlying baseline project. The baseline project was a typical software project undertaken by the user organisation as part of its normal business and the results of the experiment should therefore be replicable.

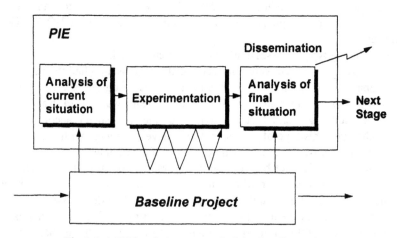

**Fig. 1.5** A PIE in relation to an underlying baseline project

The introduction of a Configuration Management System, improvements to the design documentation system, the use of a Computer Aided Design (CAD) tool, the application of Object Oriented Programming techniques, the development of a library for software re-use and the introduction of metrics, are some examples of possible improvement steps for Software Best Practice and the focus of a PIE.

It was expected that a PIE was carried out as part of a larger movement within the user organisation towards process improvement. Participants were expected to have considered their strengths and weaknesses, and to have at least an idea of the general actions required. They also needed to demonstrate that they were aware of quality issues and were considering the people aspects of their actions.

Dissemination of the results of the experiment, from a software engineering and business point of view, to the wider community, was an essential aspect of a PIE and was undertaken with the support of the Software Best Practice Dissemination Actions.

### 1.7.3    Application Experiments[4]

These experiments were targeted at building up a comprehensive set of examples to show that the adoption of improved software development practices were both possible and had clear industrial benefits. The experiments involved the introduction of state-of-the-art software engineering (e.g. management practices, methodologies, tools) into real production environments that address specific applications, and then evaluating the resulting impact.

Within the context of this book (and the project EUREX) these Application Experiments have been treated like PIEs, i.e. their specific results have been included.

### 1.7.4    Dissemination Actions[5, 6]

Dissemination Actions aimed at raising awareness and promoting the adoption of software best practice by Industry at large. Actions provided software producing organisations with information concerning the practical introduction of software best practice, how it can contribute to meeting business needs and how those organisations can benefit: particularly, by showing the real life business benefits – and costs – in a way which could be of interest to companies intending to address related problems.

The Dissemination Actions widely disseminated Software Best Practice information by making it available and packaging it in a form suitable for "focused target audiences":

- The experience gained by the participants in PIEs (Process Improvement Experiments): experiences and lessons learned which could be of interest to industry at large.
- Software Best Practice material and experiences available world-wide. For example, valuable and generally useful software engineering material which is representative of a class of processes, methodologies, assessment methods, tools, etc. Relevant world-wide experiences.

---

[4]  Application Experiments have only been called in 1993. See also the footnote to Process Improvement Experiments.
[5]  Dissemination Actions have been called in 1993, 1995 and 1996.
[6]  The ESSI project EUREX which resulted in this book was such a Dissemination Action.

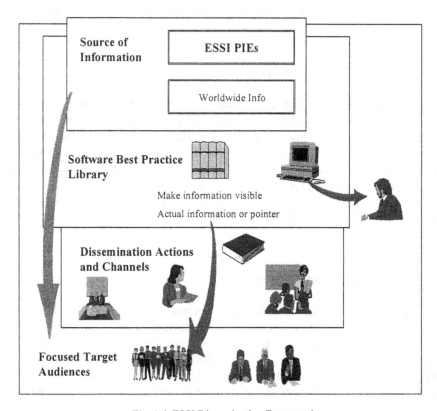

Fig. 1.6  ESSI Dissemination Framework

## 1.7.5  Experience/User Networks[7]

There was opportunity for networks of users, with a common interest, to pursue a specific problem affecting the development or use of software. Experience/User Networks mobilised groups of users at a European level and provided them with the critical mass necessary to influence their suppliers and the future of the software industry through the formulation of clear requirements. A network had to be trans-national with users from more than one Member or Associated State.

By participating in an Experience/User Network, a user organisation helped to ensure that a particular problem – with which it is closely involved – is addressed and that it is able to influence the choice of proposed solution.

Software suppliers (methodologies, tools, services, etc.) and the software industry as a whole took benefit from Experience/User Networks by receiving valuable

---

[7] Experience/User Networks have only been called in 1995.

feedback on the strengths and weaknesses of their current offerings, together with information on what is additionally required in the marketplace.

## 1.7.6   Training Actions[8]

Training actions have been broad in scope and covered training, skilling and education for all groups of people involved – directly or indirectly – in the development of software. In particular, training actions aimed at:

- increasing the awareness of senior managers as to the benefits of software process improvement and software quality
- providing software development professionals with the necessary skills to develop software using best practice

Emphasis had been placed on actions which served as a catalyst for further training and education through, for example, the training of trainers. In addition, the application of current material – where available and appropriate – in a new or wider context was preferred to the recreation of existing material.

## 1.7.7   ESSI PIE Nodes (ESPINODEs)[9]

The primary objective of an ESPINODE was to provide support and assistance, on a regional basis, to a set of PIEs in order to stimulate, support, and co-ordinate activities. ESPINODEs acted closely with local industry and were particularly aimed at helping to facilitate exchange of practical information and experience between PIEs, to provide project assistance, technical and administrative support, and to exploit synergies.

On a regional level, an ESPINODE provided a useful interface between the PIEs themselves, and between the PIEs and local industry. This included improving and facilitating access to information on ESSI/PIE results, and raising interest and awareness of local companies (notably SMEs) to the technical and business benefits resulting from software process improvement conducted in the PIEs.

At the European level, an ESPINODE exchanged information and experience with other ESPINODEs, in order to benefit from the transfer of technology, skills and know-how; from economies of scale and from synergies in general – thus creating a European network of PIE communities.

---

[8] Training Actions have been called in 1993 and 1996. Whereas the projects resulting from the call in 1996 were organised as separate projects building the ESSI Training Cluster ESSItrain, the result of the call in 1993 was one major project ESPITI which is described in chapter 2.3.2.

[9] ESSI PIE Nodes have only been called in 1997.

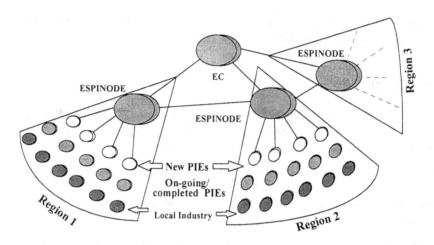

Fig. 1.7 ESPINODE collaboration model

## 1.7.8   Software Best Practice Networks (ESBNETs)[10]

The objective of an ESBNET was to implement small scale software best practice related activities on a regional basis, but within the context of a European network. A network in this context was simply a group of organisations, based in different countries, operating together to implement an ESBNET project, according to an established plan of action, using appropriate methods, technologies and other appropriate support. By operating on a regional level, it was expected that the specific needs of a targeted audience will be better addressed. The regional level was complemented by actions at European level, to exploit synergies and bring cross-fertilisation between participants and their target audiences. A network had a well defined focus, rather than being just a framework for conducting a set of unrelated, regional software best practice activities.

The two ESSI tasks newly introduced in the Call for Proposals in 1997 – ESPINODEs and ESBNETs – aimed to continue and build upon the achievements of the initiative so far, but on a more regional basis. ESPINODEs aim with first priority to provide additional support to PIEs, whilst ESBNETs aim to integrate small-scale software best practice actions of different type implemented on a regional basis – with an emphasis on the non-PIE community.

By operating on a regional level, it was expected that ESPINODEs and ESBNETs will be able to tailor their actions to the local culture, delivering the message and operating in the most appropriate way for the region. Further, it was expected that such regional actions will be able to penetrate much more into the very corners of Europe, reaching a target audience which is much broader and

---

[10] Software Best Practice Networks have only been called in 1997.

probably less experienced in dealing with European initiatives. Such an approach should be of particular interest to SMEs and other organisations not in the traditional IT sector, for which it is perhaps difficult to deal directly with an organisation based in a different country, due to – for example – a lack of resources, cultural and language reasons.

Regional Support within
European Networks

---

• **Disseminate the results
  beyond those directly
  involved in ESSI**

• **Ensure that projects act as a
  'catalyst' for further action**

• **Increase the participation in
  ESSI**

• **Reach organisations never
  involved before**

**Fig. 1.8** ESPINODEs and ESBNETs

# 2   The EUREX Project

M. Haug, E.W. Olsen
HIGHWARE, Munich

The European Experience Exchange project (EUREX) was conceived, proposed, and carried out as an ESSI Dissemination Action (see Chapter 1). The overall objective of EUREX was to evaluate the experiences of several hundred ESSI Process Improvement Experiments (PIEs) and to make this experience accessible to a broad European audience in a convenient form. In particular, the goal was to collect and make available to interested practitioners information about Software Best Practice and its introduction in specific problem domains.

In the following sections, we briefly review the history of the EUREX project.

## 2.1   Target Audience and Motivation

Over 70% of the organisations that participated in events organised during the course of the ESPITI project (see section 1.3.2 below) were Small or Medium Enterprises (SMEs), and many of which had substantially fewer than 250 employees. This response rate demonstrated a significant interest on the part of SMEs in finding out more about Software Process Improvement (SPI). Therefore, the primary target audience for EUREX was those European SMEs, and small teams in the non-IT organisations, engaged in the activity of developing software. Within these organisations, the focus was on management and technical personnel in a position to make decisions to undertake process improvement activities.

The ESPITI User Survey presents a clear picture of the needs and requirements of SMEs concerning software process improvement. For example, 25% of those who responded requested participation in working groups for experience exchange. However, SMEs are faced with many difficulties when it comes to trying to implement improvement programmes.

For example, SMEs are generally less aware than larger companies of the benefits of business-driven software process improvement. It is perceived as being an expensive task and the standard examples that are quoted in an attempt to convince them otherwise are invariably drawn from larger U.S. organisations and therefore bear little relevance for European SMEs. ESSIgram No 11 also reported that "peer review of experiment work in progress and results would be helpful."

Thus, SMEs need to see success among their peers, using moderate resources, before they are prepared to change their views and consider embarking upon SPI actions.

For those SMEs that are aware of the benefits of SPI, there are frequently other inhibitors that prevent anything useful being accomplished. Many SMEs realise that they should implement software process improvement actions but do not know how to do this. They do not have the necessary skills and knowledge to do it themselves and in many cases they do not have the financial resources to engage external experts to help them. Consequently, SPI actions get deferred or cancelled because other business priorities assume greater importance. Even those SMEs that do successfully initiate SPI programmes can find that these activities are not seen through to their natural completion stage because of operational or financial constraints.

Many of the concerns about the relevance of SPI for SMEs were addressed by EUREX in a series of workshops in which speakers from similarly characterised companies spoke about their experiences with SPI. The workshops were in integral part of the EUREX process and provided much of the data presented in this volume.

The Commission funded EUREX in large measure because the evaluation of approximately 300 PIEs was too costly for an independent endeavour. Even if some resource-rich organisation had undertaken this task, it is likely that the results would not have been disseminated, but would rather have been used to further competitive advantage. Commission support has insured that the results are widely and publicly distributed.

Many ESSI dissemination actions have been organised as conferences or workshops. PIE Users register in order to discharge their obligations to the Commission; however, the selection and qualification of contributions is often less than rigorous. In addition, many public conferences have added PIE presentation tracks with little organisation of their content. Small audiences are a consequence of the competition of that track with others in the conference. The common thread in these experiences is that organisation of the actions had been lacking or passive.

EUREX turned this model on its end. PIE Users were approached proactively to involve them in the process. In addition, the information exchange process was actively managed. The EUREX workshops were organised around several distinct problem domains and workshop attendees were supported with expert assistance to evaluate their situations and provide commentary on solutions from a broadly experienced perspective. (See chapter 3 for a detailed discussion of the domain selection process.) Participants were invited through press publications, the local chambers of commerce, the Regional Organisations of EUREX and through cooperation with other dissemination actions.

This approach provided a richer experience for attendees. Since the workshops were domain-oriented, the participants heard different approaches to the same issues and were presented with alternative experiences and solutions. This was a more informative experience than simply hearing a talk about experiences in a vacuum, with no background and no possibility for comparison or evaluation. The opportunity to exchange views with one's peers and to hear advice from respected experts provides substantial benefit not found using a passive approach to dissemination.

Our approach also offered a better experience for European Industry as a whole. Since we have categorised and evaluated approximately 300 different improvement experiments, we present a broad practical view of the selected problem domains. This is distinctly different from purely academic approaches that offer little practical experience. EUREX is an opportunity to derive additional benefit from the PIEs, beyond that of obligatory presentations. We hope to lend an authoritative voice to the overall discussion of Software Process Improvement.

## 2.2 Objectives and Approach

As mentioned above, the objective of EUREX was to assess, classify, categorise, and exploit the experience of the ESSI PIE Prime Users and Associated Partners (collectively referred to here simply as Users or PIE Users) and then to make this experience accessible. In particular, we sought to provide a broad European audience with data about Software Best Practice and its introduction in selected problem domains.

The approach is broken down into two phases. The first phase required the classification and collection of data and the second phase involves the analysis, distribution and dissemination of the resulting information. The phases were implemented in three steps:

1. Classify and categorise the base of PIE Users and the Problem Domains addressed by them. All of the available material from over 300 PIEs was assessed, the categorisation was designed such that over 90% of the material under consideration fell into one of the selected Problem Domains (see chapter 3).
2. Plan and conduct a series of Regional Workshops in order to collect information from PIE projects as well as for disseminating the PIE's experiences at a regional level. 18 workshops in 8 European countries were undertaken. (Refer to chapter 7 for the best of the workshop material.)
3. Publish the first four of the Software Best Practice Reports and Executive Reports to detail the experiences. In addition, a Web-site provides access to the background material used by EUREX.

Steps 1 and 2 fall within phase one and steps 2 and 3 are within phase two. Notice that, because multiple benefits are derived from the same activity, the two phases overlapped somewhat. This approach is intended to convey to the largest possible audience the experiences of the Commission's Process Improvement Experiment program.

The EUREX Software Best Practice Reports (of which this volume is one) and Executive Reports are directed at two distinct audiences. The first is the technically oriented IT manager or developer interested in the full reports and technology background. The second is senior management, for whom the Executive Reports a summary of benefits and risks of real cases are appropriate.

## 2.3   Partners

The EUREX project was carried out by the following partners:

- HIGHWARE GmbH, Germany (Coordinator)
- Editions HIGHWARE sarl, France
- GEMINI Soc. Cons. A, Italy
- SOCINTEC, Spain
- SISU, Sweden
- MARI Northern Ireland Ltd., United Kingdom.

The fact that MARI has left the consortium (as they did with other projects as well) caused some disruption and delay for the project. The partners were able to compensate largely, e.g. the number of workshops held and the countries covered. Even the book about the domain assigned to MARI, Object Orientation, was prepared with the help of FZI Forschungszentrum Informatik, Karlsruhe, Germany.

## 2.4   Related Dissemination and Training Actions

Other ESSI Dissemination Actions that have also generated significant results that may be of interest to the reader. These actions include SISSI and ESPITI, both described briefly below.

### 2.4.1   Software Improvement Case Studies Initiative (SISSI)

European companies must face the challenge of translating software engineering into a competitive advantage in the market place, by taking full advantage of the existing experiences and results. The process of overcoming existing barriers is not an easy one, particularly if individual companies must face them on their own. It is a major issue to put at the disposal of companies a set of written case studies providing a practical view of software process improvement (SPI) impact and best practices. Successful experiences can demonstrate that existing barriers can be dismantled. This learning process, which takes time and requires continuity in the long term, is being fostered by the SISSI project.

### 2.4.1.1 Overview

The target audience for the SISSI case studies is senior executives, i.e. decision-makers, in software producing organisations through Europe. This includes both software vendors and companies developing software for in-house use. The material has been selected in such a way that it is relevant for both small and large organisations.

SISSI produced a set of 33 case studies, of about 4 pages each, and distributed 50 case studies overall, together with cases from previous projects. Cases are not exclusively technical; rather, they have a clear business orientation and are focused on action. Cases are a selected compendium of finished Process Improvement Experiments (PIEs) funded by the ESSI program of the EC. They are classified according to parameters and keywords so tailored and selective extractions can be made by potential users or readers. The main selection criteria are the business sector, the software process affected by the improvement project and its business goals.

The dissemination mechanisms of SISSI were the following: a selective telephone-led campaign addressed to 500 appropriate organisations together with follow up actions; an extensive mailing campaign targeting 5000 additional organisations which have selected the relevant cases from an introductory document; joint action with the European Network of SPI Nodes – ESPINODEs – to distribute the SISSI material and provide continuity to the SISSI project; WWW pages with the full contents of the case studies; synergic actions with other Dissemination Actions of the ESSI initiative, like EUREX, SPIRE, RAPID; co-operation with other agents like European publications, SPI institutions, or graduate studies acting as secondary distribution channels.

SISSI developed an SPI Marketing Plan to systematically identify and access this target market in any European country and distributed its contents through the European Network of SPI Nodes both for a secondary distribution of SISSI Case Studies, and for a suitable rendering of the ESPINODEs services. The plan was implemented for the dissemination of the SISSI Case Studies in several European countries, proving its validity.

### 2.4.1.2 Objectives

The main goals of the approach taken in the SISSI project have been as follows:

- The material produced has been formed by a wide variety of practical real cases selected by the consultants of the consortium, and documented in a friendly and didactic way to capture interest between companies.
- The cases have clearly emphasised the key aspects of the improvement projects in terms of competitive advantage and tangible benefits (cost, time to market, quality).

- Most of the cases have been successful cases, but also not successful ones have been sought in order to analyse causes of failure, i.e. inadequate analysis of the plan before starting the project.
- The project has not been specially focused on particular techniques or application areas, but it has been a selected compendium of the current and finished Process Improvement Experiments – PIEs –. They have been classified according to different parameters and keywords so tailored and selective extractions can be made by potential users or readers. The main selection criteria have been: business sector (finance, electronics, manufacturing, software houses, engineering, etc.), the software process, the business goals and some technological aspects of the experiment.
- The Dissemination action should open new markets promoting the SPI benefits in companies not already contacted by traditional ESSI actions.
- The SISSI Marketing Plan should provide the methodology and the information not only to disseminate the SISSI material, but has to be generic enough to direct the marketing of other ESSI services and SPI activities in general.

The SISSI material should be used in the future by organisations and other dissemination actions and best practices networks as a reference material to guide lines of software improvement and practical approaches to face them. In particular, SISSI has to provide continuity of the action beyond the project itself supporting the marketing of SPI in any other ESSI action.


## 2.4.2  ESPITI

The European Software Process Improvement Training Initiative (ESPITI) was officially launched on 22 November 1994 in Belfast, Northern Ireland. The final event was held in Berlin, Germany in Spring 1996. The Initiative aimed to maximise the benefits gained from European activities in the improvement and subsequent ISO 9000 certification of the software development process through training. A sum of 8.5 million ECU was allocated to the Initiative for a period of 18 months, to support actions intended to:

- Identify the true needs of European industry for training in software process improvement (SPI).
- Increase the level of awareness of the benefits of software process improvement and ISO 9001.
- Provide training for trainers, managers and software engineers.
- Support the development of networks between organisations at regional and European levels to share knowledge and experience and form links of mutual benefit.
- Liase with similar initiatives world-wide and transfer their experiences to Europe.

### 2.4.2.1   Organisational Structure

The Initiative was implemented through a network of 14 Regional Organisations addressing the local needs of 17 EU and EFTA countries. Regional Organisations (ROs) have been existing commercial organisations that were contracted to carry out a specific range of activities in support of the ESPITI goals. The ROs were divided into 2 sets, each set supported by a Partner. The two Partner organisations, Forschungszentrum Karlsruhe GmbH from Germany and MARI (Northern Ireland) Ltd from the United Kingdom, have been co-ordinating and supporting co-operation at European level through the provision of services to the ROs. These services included provision of:

- Preparation of a user survey in all countries involved to determine the local SPI needs.
- An electronic communication network for exchanging SPI information of mutual interest.
- Guidelines on event organisation, e.g. seminars, training courses and working groups.
- Awareness material for project launches, software process improvement and ISO 9001.
- Assistance in evaluating performance at project and event levels.
- Guidance in programme planning and control.
- Assistance in PR activities.
- Assistance in experience exchange and co-operation between the ROs.

The European Software Institute ESI was also involved in ESPITI, providing the Partners with valuable assistance, including the merging of the European user survey results, liaison with other initiatives and contributions to RO meetings.

### 2.4.2.2   The ESPITI Approach

The ESPITI project adopted a multi-pronged strategy for improving the competitiveness of the European software industry.

- Survey of European needs was carried out to ascertain the needs and the best approach to adopt to satisfy these needs within each region.
- Seminars for raising awareness of the benefits and approaches to quality management and process improvement.
- Training courses for improving know-how in initiating, assessing, planning and implementing quality management and process improvement programmes.
- Workshops, which aim to teach participants about a subject and direct them in implementing the subject in their Organisations.
- Working groups for enabling dissemination of experience in a subject, and to allow participants to discuss and learn about those experiences.
- Case studies for demonstrating the successes and difficulties in software process improvement.

- Liaisons with similar, related initiatives world-wide to understand their approaches and successes and to transfer the lessons learned there to Europe.
- Public relations activities to promote the aims and objectives of ESPITI and to ensure participation in ESPITI events.
- Evaluation of the ESPITI project to assess the effectiveness of the initiative, and to determine how the initiative could progress from there.

### 2.4.2.3    The Partners and Regional Organisations

#### The Partners

- MARI (Northern Ireland) Ltd, United Kingdom
- Forschungszentrum Karlsruhe GmbH, Germany

#### The Regional Organisations

- Austrian Research Centre, Austria
- Flemish Quality Management Centre, Belgium
- Delta Software Engineering, Denmark
- CCC Software Professionals Oy, Finland
- AFNOR, France
- Forschungszentrum Karlsruhe GmbH, Germany
- INTRASOFT SA, Greece
- University of Iceland, Iceland
- Centre for Software Engineering, Ireland
- ETNOTEAM, Italy
- Centre de Recherche Public Henri Tudor, Luxembourg
- SERC, The Netherlands
- Norsk Regnesentral, Norway
- Instituto Portugues da Qualidade, Portugal
- Sip Consultoría y formación, Spain
- SISU, Sweden
- MARI (Northern Ireland) Ltd., United Kingdom

# 3 The EUREX Taxonomy

M. Haug, E.W. Olsen
HIGHWARE, Munich

One of the most significant tasks performed during the EUREX project was the creation of the taxonomy needed to drive the Regional Workshops and, ultimately, the content of these Software Best Practice Reports. In this chapter, we examine in detail the process that led to the EUREX taxonomy and discuss how the taxonomy led to the selection of PIEs for the specific subject domain.

## 3.1 Analysis and Assessment of PIEs

Over 300 Process Improvement Experiments (PIEs) funded by the Commission in the calls of 1993, 1995 and 1996 were analysed using an iterative approach as described below. The technical domain of each of the PIEs was assessed by EUREX and each PIE was attributed to certain technological areas.

Early discussions proved what others (including the Commission) had already experienced in the attempt to classify PIEs: there is no canonical, "right" classification. The type, scope and detail of a classification depends almost entirely on the intended use for the classification. The EUREX taxonomy was required to serve the EUREX project. In particular, it was used to drive the selection of suitable subject areas for the books and, consequently, the selection of regional workshop topics to insure that good coverage would be achieved both by the number of PIEs and by the partners in their respective regions.

## 3.2 Classification into Problem Domains

A set of more than 150 attributes was refined in several iterations to arrive at a coarse grain classification into technological problem domains. These domains were defined such that the vast majority of PIEs fall into at least one of these domains. There were seven steps used in the process of discovering the domains, as described in the following paragraphs.

In part because of the distributed nature of the work and in part because of the necessity for several iterations, the classification required 6 calendar months to complete.

### 3.2.1   First Regional Classification

Each partner examined the PIEs conducted within its region and assigned attributes from the list given above that described the work done within the PIE (more than one attribute per PIE was allowed). The regions were assigned as shown in Table 3.1.

Table 3.1 Regional responsibilities of consortium partners

| Partner | Region |
| --- | --- |
| SISU | Denmark, Finland, Norway, Sweden |
| MARI | United Kingdom, Ireland |
| GEMINI | Italy |
| SOCINTEC | Spain, Portugal, Greece |
| HIGHWARE Germany | Germany, Austria, The Netherlands, Israel and all other regions not explicitly assigned |
| HIGHWARE France | Benelux, France |

### 3.2.2   Result of First Regional Classification

HIGHWARE Germany (the consortium co-ordinator) began with a classification of the German PIEs according to the above procedure. This first attempt was distributed among the partners as a working example.

Using the example, each partner constructed a spreadsheet with a first local classification and returned this to HIGHWARE Germany.

### 3.2.3   Consolidation and Iteration

HIGHWARE Germany prepared a consolidated spreadsheet using the partners' input, and developed from that a first classification and clustering proposal. This was sent to the other partners for review and cross-checking.

### 3.2.4   Update of Regional Classification

All partners reviewed their classification, in particular the assignment of attributes to PIEs. Corrections were made as necessary.

### 3.2.5 Mapping of Attributes

HIGHWARE Germany mapped all key words used by the partners into a new set of attributes, normalising the names of attributes. No attribute was deleted, but the overall number of different attributes decreased from 164 to 127. These attributes were further mapped into classes and subclasses that differentiate members of classes. This second mapping lead to a set of 24 classes each containing 0 to 13 subclasses. The resulting classes are shown in table 3.2.

**Table 3.2** Attributes of the Classification

| | | |
|---|---|---|
| Assessment | Case Tools | Change Management |
| Configuration Management | Decision Support | Documentation |
| Estimation | Formal Methods | Life Cycle: Analysis & Design |
| Life Cycle: Dynamic System Modelling | Life Cycle: Installation & Maintenance | Life Cycle: Requirements & Specification |
| Life Cycle: Product Management. | Metrics | Modelling & Simulation |
| Object Orientation | Process Model: Definition | Process Model: Distributed |
| Process Model: Iterative | Process Model: Support | Project Management |
| Prototyping | Quality Management | Reengineering |
| Reuse & Components | Reverse Engineering | Target Environment |
| Testing, Verification & Validation | User Interface | |

### 3.2.6 Review of Classification and Mapping into Subject Domains

The classification achieved by the above mentioned process was reviewed by the partners and accepted with minor adjustments. It is important to note that up to this point, the classification was independent of the structure of the planned publications. It simply described the technical work done by PIEs in the consolidated view of the project partners.

In the next step this view was discussed and grouped into subject domains suitable for publications planned by the consortium.

### 3.2.7 Subject Domains Chosen

Out of the original 24 classes, 7 were discarded from the further consideration, either because the number of PIEs in the class was not significant or because the domain was already addressed by other ESSI Dissemination Actions (e.g. formal methods, reengineering, and so on). The 17 final classes were grouped into the subject domains shown in table 3.3 such that each of the resulting 5 domains forms a suitable working title for one of the EUREX books.

**Table 3.3** Final Allocation of Domains

| Partner | Domain |
|---|---|
| SISU | Metrics, Measurement and Process Modelling |
| MARI | Object Orientation, Reuse and Components |
| GEMINI | Testing, Verification, Validation, Quality Management |
| SOCINTEC | Configuration & Change Management, Requirements Engineering |
| HIGHWARE France | Project Management, Estimation, Life Cycle Support |

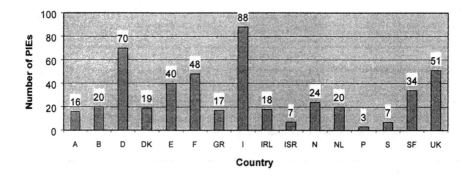

**Fig. 3.1** All PIEs by Country

The breakdown of all (unclassified) PIEs on a per-country basis is shown in Fig. 3.1. The distribution of PIEs is somewhat related to population, but there are notable exceptions (e.g. Italy and France).

The classification breakdown of PIEs Europe-wide is worth examining. Referring to Fig. 3.2, notice first that the classification has resulted in a relatively even distribution of projects, only the Project Management classification dips noticeably below the average. The number of PIEs without any classification was held below 10% of the total. (Further discussion of the "No Classification" category appears below.)

### 3.2.8 Unclassified PIEs

There we 33 PIEs that were not classified by EUREX. There were generally two reasons for lack of classification.

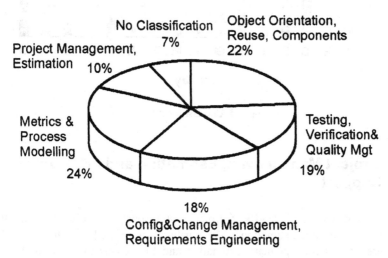

Fig. 3.2 Classification of PIEs Europe-wide

1. Neither the EUREX reviewer alone nor the consortium as a whole was able to reach a conclusion for classification based on the PIE description as published.
2. The PIE addressed a very specific subject that did not correspond to a class defined by EUREX and/or the PIE was dealt with by other known ESSI projects, e.g. formal methods. The consortium tried to avoid too much overlap with other projects.

When one of these rules was applied, the corresponding PIE was given no classification and was not considered further by the EUREX analysis. Fig. 3.3 shows the breakdown of unclassified PIEs by country.

As can be seen in Fig. 3.3, there were 33 PIEs that remained unclassified once the EUREX analysis was complete.

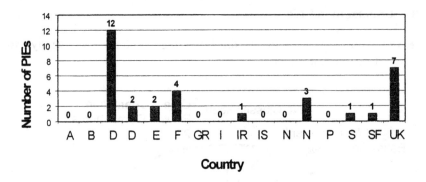

Fig. 3.3 Unclassified PIEs.

## 3.3   Project Management, Estimation and Life Cycle Support

Part II presents the results of EUREX project with respect to the classification "Project Management and Estimation". The attributes associated with this classification were Project Management, Estimation and Life Cycle Support. Within this classification there were a total of 47 PIEs that were assigned one or more of these attributes. The distribution of these PIEs throughout Europe is shown in figure 3.4.

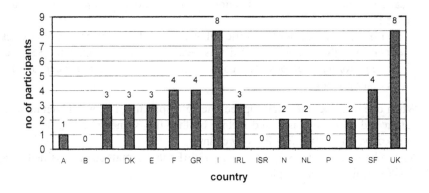

Fig. 3.4 Distribution of PIEs classified for the domain

# Part II

# Project Management, Estimation and Life Cycle Support

# 4 Perspectives

G. Vallet
Editions HIGHWARE, Paris

The French EUREX team was responsible for the domain classified as Project Management and this volume discusses the results obtained by EUREX concerning this domain.

This chapter provides an introduction to the central theme of the domain and presents two expert contributions that provide interesting perspectives on project management. Arnold Rochfeld discusses the software life cycle and related methodologies. Adrian Cowderoy and Fred Schindler present best practices in estimation and risk management.

## 4.1 The Domain Subject

A project is a set of actions whose combined goal is to achieve a defined result. This result is what we call the product. The product must be well-defined and understood prior to the start of the project and the definition needs to remain stable over the lifetime of the project. It must be possible to measure that the product is complete.

Rules and techniques exist to define and plan a project and then to lead it (it means to bring it to its end i.e. the product delivery). The "project mode" is built from this set of rules and techniques.

Of course, "all is not project": Not all rules and techniques of the project mode need to be used for each and every activity.

To lead a project means to ensure that the conditions needed to complete the project are present and to make corrections when necessary.

The mechanism of "project tracking" (see Figure 4.1) measures the lag or difference between the real route and the planned route (used as a baseline) and is fundamental to project leadership.

These components are integral to project management:

- Baseline: A project is split into intermediate tasks that, taken together, lead to the final product. The intermediate tasks and products are listed in a project development plan.

Fig. 4.1 Purpose of project tracking

- Schedule: The project schedule defines the order and the technical logic of the intermediate deliveries.
- Project Tracking: The tracking process is based on regular and periodic progress reviews.

Each progress review consists of:
- An analysis of all the tasks in progress at each progress point;
- The interpretation of this analysis to set a value to the progress of the project;

A new prediction for project completion obtained consolidating all of the individual predictions for the tasks in progress (a revised schedule).

Eventually, a new schedule (an example is given on Figure 4.2) can show that the project place is not being met. There is a need for arbitration.

To prepare for arbitration, the following technique is often used. It consists of building following index (see figure 4.3):

- The first bar is a model of the schedule obtained with the resources available for the project.
- A second bar represents the schedule obtained with unlimited resource.

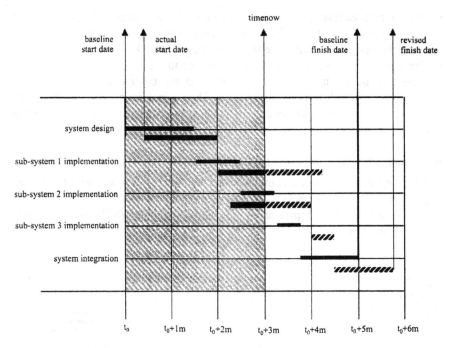

**Fig. 4.2** A typical progress report

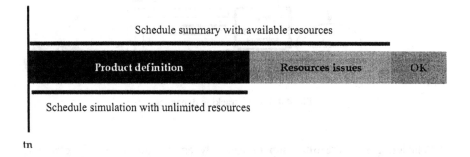

**Fig. 4.3** Project scheduling and management issues

The right-most ends of these two bars divide the future in three areas:

- The right area (light grey) is also named the green area. If the contractual date of the end of the project is located in this area, there is no need for additional action.

- The central area (dark grey) is the orange area. If the contractual date of the end of the project is located in this area, it means that the contractual date will not be reached but could be if more resources are given to the project.
- The left area (black) is the red area. If the contractual date of the end of the project is located in this area, it means that the contractual date cannot be achieved even with unlimited resources. The project definition must be modified (at least, the completion date must be updated). This is a problem for the product manager.

A project mode is a periodic, dynamic process (see Figure 4.4) run in two steps:

- First step answers the question: "Where are the projects and where are they going with current assumptions?"
- Second step is set to prepare arbitration: it may involve modifying the assumptions of the project.

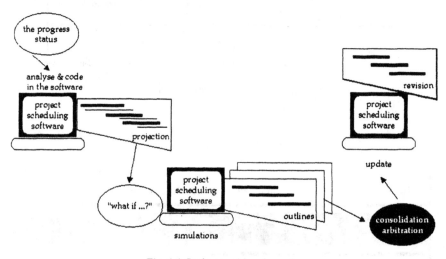

**Fig. 4.4** Project tracking dynamics

Scheduling software often supports this dynamic process. See Chapter 5 for some references to tools designed for this purpose.

The implementation of the project mode in a company is to use the process described above to manage projects. This implementation process may encounter three types of risks:

- Effort consuming
- Too far away from reality
- Unused progress reports

The main risks factors are shown in table 4.1.

**Table 4.1** Risks related to their factors

| Risk | Risk Factor |
| --- | --- |
| Effort consuming | Too detailed |
|  | Scheduling techniques are unknown |
|  | Tool complexity |
|  | Overloaded project leader |
| Too far away from reality | Inadequate plan |
|  | Reluctance to be controlled |
| Unused progress report | Scheduling techniques are unknown |
|  | Progress metrics is not understood |
|  | Project management poorly organised |

Figure 4.5 shows some preventive actions used to reduce the risks.

- Training actions are used once for each resource;
- Consultancy actions are employed once for each project;
- Support actions are used throughout the life of the project.

Planning practices are fundamental to the project mode:

- The decision to realise – or not – a project is based on the estimations of the time and the costs necessary to do it. Once a project is started, an important factor of success is how the project was planned. Indeed, project management techniques and tools are based upon comparing a current status with a nominal one, namely the baseline.
- A critical issue is to set a realistic baseline. Realistic both qualitatively and quantitatively. Some tools are described in chapter 5 that support methods for Software Development.

Qualitative realism is achieved by the formalisation of the project process, while quantitative realism is accomplished by estimation and arbitration.

| | project planner | project leader | project owner | director | product manager | product owner |
|---|---|---|---|---|---|---|
| Too detailed | know pjct planning techniques | improve pjct planning practice | awareness of pjct planning techniques | | | |
| Scheduling techniques are unknown | know pjct scheduling techniques | know pjct scheduling techniques | know resrce scheduling techniques | | know pjct scheduling techniques | |
| Tool complexity | know operating mode | know tool settings | define tool settings | | | |
| Overloaded project leader | operate project office | use project office | set up project office | | | |
| Inadequate plan | | improve pjct planning practice | review pjct contract | | improve pjct planning practice | review project plan |
| Reluctance to be controlled | provide feedback | track mile-stones | organize information flows | focus on objectives | | |
| Progress metrics is not understood | know project metrics | define pjct progress metrics | define std pjct progress metrics | | define pjct progress metrics | |
| Prjct management poorly organised | provide reports in time | operate progress reviews | operate multi-pjct reviews | set the rules of the game | control change requests | Approve pjct manage-ment |

**Fig. 4.5** Project tracking dynamics

## 4.2   Software Life Cycle

Arnold Rochfeld
AR Consultants, Paris

Arnold Rochfeld is a consultant in Information System Design and in Information System Development. He has more than 20 years of experience, both in public services and in important private firms. He was involved in strategic plans, in requirements studies and especially in data and process modelling and in architecture modelling. He was the main designer of the Merise methodology, the most used Information System Design methodology in French speaking countries.

Arnold Rochfeld teaches Information System Design in the Conservatoire des Arts et Metiers Paris, the Ecole des Mines de Paris, Télécom Paris, and in the Lyon 3 University.

Arnold Rochfeld is the author of several books and articles about Information System Design with Merise and OOM.

## 4.2.1   Relevant Standards

For a long time, the Software Life Cycle was reduced to an unique life cycle, the Software Development Life Cycle. Recently, the Software Life Cycle is seen as a more complex system, which combines co-operative processes (primary and associated processes). The American standard ISO 12207 proposes a coherent vision of such a system. The primary process or main process covers the most significant activities of software production, such as:

- software acquisition (customer side of a project),
- software supply (supplier side of a project),
- software production,
- software operation.

Each of these elementary processes is seen as a set of tasks or other relevant subdivisions (phases, steps).

Associated processes include the support process and the organisational process.

The Support process deals with activities such as:

- documentation,
- configuration management,
- quality assurance,
- verification, validation, review, audit and problem resolution.

The Organisational process deals with activities such as:

- project management,
- infrastructure management covering development infrastructure (case tools, programming languages) and communication infrastructure (CORBA, RMI, Com, MQ Series,…)
- improvement management,
- training of a project team or software users.

SAPHIR, a French standard promoted by an organisation of software houses (Syntec), brings up an interesting complement to software production. Following SDM/S, the process management methodology of the 70's and the 80's, SAPHIR stresses that any project is based on three main phases, i.e.:

- preparation or project launching where the nature of a mission and requirements to be meet are defined through management and user interviews,
- development or project production activity where tasks related to a relevant subdivision are effectively performed,

- ending which is concretised by the effective production of "contractual" documents, which allow the evaluation of the quality of the project production.

Therefore, a project management methodology must include, the following steps:
- Requirements definition and analysis, similar to the preparation phase,
- Design and implementation, similar to the production phase,
- Deployment, which constitutes the normal end of any given project.

These steps are decomposed into tasks. They are supposed to produce, among other things, tangible results to allow a decision to be taken at the end of each subdivision, i. e.:
- to continue if the produced results are conform to decision maker's expectation,
- to redo or to improve the results, if the produced results need to be changed, without any fundamental transformation of the initial mission,
- to stop the course of the ongoing subdivision, if the produced results imply fundamental redefinition of the initial mission.

Each of these phases must include support process considerations. For instance, tangible results must allow verification, validation, and review, according to a defined quality assurance plan. Associated documentation must be produced.

SAPHIR includes the definitions of specific tasks devoted to the customer and to the supplier sides of projects, definitions which are close to software acquisition and software supply processes depicted above. The standard defines also seven generic tasks assigned to any given project leader, in accordance with ISO 12207 standard. These tasks are:

1. Strategic follow-up or permanent follow-up of the domain project coverage, to make sure that the customer side project objectives are taken properly into account, and that the project doesn't deviate from the original project,
2. Operational management, the core of project leader activity, which deals with resource management, planning and ordering of tasks, problem resolution.
3. Organisation aspects: good organisation structures set-up which will facilitate project steps,
4. Improvement management whose aim is the effective utilisation of project results and which supposes proper user organisation, adequate training, follow-up, migration from legacy Information System to the new Information System,
5. Contractual management: management of relationships with external entities, users and sub-contractors, as far as management of relationship between supply side and customer side of the project,
6. Quality management which covers quality definition and follow-up, all measures which will guarantee the quality of the results of a project,
7. Operation management which covers production means, choice of proper computer professionals and good usage of them.

These three phases and seven tasks are the core of any project management methodology and constitute the backbone of any Software Life Cycle.

### 4.2.2   Effects of Object Orientation on Software Life Cycle

The above topics remain true when Object orientation are used, even if the nature of the tangible results has changed. Given subdivisions may stay as such but generally the steps are now based on an incremental development cycle using a set of prototypes.

Object oriented methodologies makes use of a set of models (or diagrams) such as:

- Functional model (Use Cases diagrams or Data Flow Diagrams), showing system functionality and system breakthroughs,
- Class and Object models or classes and object diagrams, showing classes definition, constraints on attributes, on relationship between classes, classes hierarchies (classes and subclasses), classes aggregation-composed objects,
- ...

In most cases, such models or diagrams are based on Entity-Relationship concepts.

Dynamic models showing elementary (collaboration diagram) and detailed collaboration (activity diagram) between objects, objects life cycle (statechart diagrams, state transitions formal definition), usage of messages and objects according to Use Cases or scenarios (Sequence diagrams).

Theoretical bases come mostly from Petri nets theory.

Architectural models only limited to components and the deployment of technical objects diagrams or including the organisational model of deployment (sites of deployment, their functions and their actors), as well as a model of computer processes, software and infrastructure components, etc.

Such models could be more or less formal and based on slightly different graphical conventions.

In Europe, especially in France, such models are based on a specific Life Cycle of Abstractions, which offers three level of definition, i. e.

- a Conceptual level, where functions of the Information System – IS – and data are defined at the Enterprise level, without any organisational or technical considerations,
- a Logical level where a technical target is chosen, as far as data organisation (Relational DBMS, OO DBMS, ...) and programming language type (OOPL – C++, Java – , Cobol,...) are concerned,
- a Physical level, where a specific DBMS and a specific PL is chosen.

Architectural models may also include organisational considerations.

In most countries (especially in the US), such Abstractions Life Cycle is limited to two levels, physical and logical, and everything which is not physical is considered as logical.

A specific software life cycle will make used of a Planning study, of short duration defining:

- critical Success Factors to be met by applications; business opportunities produced by new technology (Object orientations, network, ...),
- alternate Technical Architectures to be used. At this level, a limited architectural model can be build. A first infrastructure prototype showing for critical technical architectures their capacity to support distributed and customer oriented applications may be produced,
- a realistic Development plan.

Infrastructure management aspects are of great importance at this level. And so are improvement and project management aspects. Training of designers needed by future steps are here of great importance.

A Feasibility or a Preliminary study of the project, producing a balance between costs and advantages of distinct development scenarios and showing ROI – Return on Investment – of each. Such a study will produce at least a functional model of the planned system and of system breakthroughs. But it can also be more complete, and include the whole set of models presented above but limited to a significant subset of the Information System. A preliminary prototype can be also produced. If such is the case, physical models must be specified and a limited implementation performed.

This step is optional but must be done if a important evolution of the enterprise is expected. For instance, it is the case when entry in e-market, or in e-Banking is intended. It is also very helpful, if the use of ERP is planned, to define the borders between developed functions and ERP functions. It is a direct reference to Improvement management dealt with by the Organisational process.

A Detailed study where all models are produced, specially at conceptual and logical levels. Scenarios are specified and so are the Graphical User Interfaces.

A GUI prototype can be implemented. Its intended objective is to show to potential users, the interfaces and their main characteristics (friendliness, menus, breakthroughs, attributes).

A Technical study devoted to technical considerations (component breakthroughs, definition of common design patterns, physical model of classes and of Support Data Base, optimisation of links between objects). Such study concentrates about the physical level of the planned solution. An Industrialisation prototype can be proposed, allowing the measurement of physical performances of the planned solution.

At the end of such a study, a comprehensive approach must be performed, as far as IS components are concerned. It will define:

- which components will be implemented,
- which components will be acquired outside,
- which components will be reused, eventually with extended functionality or improved performances.

This view is a concrete result of improvement management as covert by Organisational process.

Planning of training of project team, involved in Implementation phase, are here of great importance.

An Implementation phase, where the system or the subsystem is implemented, giving way to a usable Prototype, partial or total, open to experiment by real users.

All results expected from the support process are here very important.

A Deployment phase, where the computer system or subsystem is deliver to users and deploy on several sites.

Documentation and configuration management aspects must be treated.

Several prototypes of each kind can be defined, giving way to a real implementation spiral methodology, indicating risks taken and expected benefits on the client side of the project. EUROMETHOD has defined a risks taxonomy:

- stability of information and business processes,
- stability of the IS,
- development technology risks,
- non-functional requirements of the computer system – ergonomic aspects, communication –
- project duration and delays, schedule adequacy,
- ...

which helps to determine the number of needed prototypes. They allow a very flexible management of the Improvement process. Object orientation facilitates the production of economical prototypes, by reuse of objects.

Such an approach will minimise the Information System time to market, will provide a good ROS – Return On Specification – and will offer good visibility for users, since each step provides a possible prototype to them.

These changes in standards and technology are an important support of Process Improvement Experiment. They are important factors of improvement.


## 4.3   Best Practices in Estimation

A. Cowderoy
The Multimedia House of Quality Limited

F. Schindler
Philotech GmbH, München


Adrian Cowderoy is managing director of the Multimedia House of Quality, and has provided project-management support and industrial training courses on quality management, cost estimation and risk management to the aerospace and medical industries across Europe, and in India, Japan, and the USA. He is a visiting lecturer at City University, London, teaching project management for systems development, and at Middlesex University on e-commerce projects.

He was project manager and technical director of the EU's MultiSpace project, creator of the Goal Risk Tool, and has been involved in development and coordination of .EU projects for 12 years. He chaired the ESCOM conferences from 1996-1999, and is the coordinator for the Metrics Week 2000 (IEEE Metrics and ESCOM). He has published on quality and project management, and is a registered expert to the European Commission DGXIII. He is a founding member of NexusWorld.

Adrian Cowderoy received a MSc in Management Science from Imperial College, University of London, and a BSc from Queen Mary College, London. He spent the first 6 years of his career as a quality consultant and software developer at International Computers Limited, UK.

Fred Schindler is head of the IT-department of philotech GmbH, Munich, a company active in the area of software development for technical application. He has been involved in many software projects requiring highest quality standards for the Aerospace and Defence Industry as software developer; consultant for quality and process improvement and as project manager. Cost and effort estimation, risk management and process improvement for small and medium sized companies belong to his main fields of interest.

## Introduction

There is a conundrum for many software development departments and companies. To be profitable or effective, projects must address new challenges, under difficult conditions. Such projects encounter risk factors from these new challenges and difficult conditions. These risk factors can exaggerate the differences from previous projects, making it difficult to estimate project duration, effort and cost. Worse, project margins are so tight that under-estimates can easily cause financial losses, while competition for projects and funds is so severe that an over-estimate can result in a lost contract.

This chapter shows hidden strengths of modern estimation methods. The chapter explains how estimation is used in the context of different types of project and organisation. This leads to a statement of best practice for estimation in different types of organisation, and some common examples of worst practice.

The inspiration for the chapter came from experiences of the ESSI project CO-COSPIE, which introduced estimation and sizing methods into a small company that specialises in developing high reliability real-time systems. However the chapter also uses many years of accumulated experiences from introducing estimation to a broad range of communities across Europe.

### 4.3.1 Principles of Estimation

An estimate is a prediction of value that will be measured later, but can not yet be measured. (For example, the duration and resource cost of a project and its tasks may be estimated at the start of the project, then estimated again after each phase is completed).

All estimation methods rely on only a few basic strategies, sometimes combining them:

- Analogy involves identifying the most similar previous project or task.
- Case-based reasoning involves taking a stereotypical or especially relevant task, and estimating the consequences of the differences.
- Comparison with previous local projects. which typically involves some form of statistical analysis, but alternative exist via the Delphi technique, neural nets or even genetic algorithms.
- Comparison with other projects in similar and other parts of the industry. Most commercial "cost estimation" tools are based on this strategy.

These are then combined, such as in "bottom-up" effort estimates which aggregate task effort to get project effort. Likewise "top-down" estimates typically use experiences from previous projects to subdivided total effort among the parts.

So-called "expert opinion" usually involves a combination of these methods, if it is systematic.

### 4.3.2 Hidden Strengths

Cost reduction can be even more important than cost prediction, for both the developer and the client. Ideas of how to reduce costs are needed during project proposal and tendering, when planning the project, and at every major decision point during the project. For each of these ideas, proposals are needed of how they would be achieved, their cost, and the secondary effects they may have on the project.

- This is where effort estimation models help, especially those that are embedded within easy-to-use commercial tools. The data used by the model represents a list of ideas for improvement, and the entire model is a method of assessing the impact. Some estimating tools provide detailed descriptions of the cost influences in different methods of working, different staffing options, and the impact of different design decisions.
- Analogy-based estimation also help, because it provides much more than an estimate: it highlights similarities between projects, and hence the lessons to be learned. (Case-based reasoning goes further by the features that are different.) During the proposal or planning stages of a project, these analogies and refer-

ence cases may be a major source of information about the likely design of the product.

The use of estimation methods to help with cost reduction results in another benefit. Designers and team leaders can learn more about the different influences on the project, and how these are dependent on each other. A model such as CO-COMO-II has so much detail and accumulated expertise built into it that everyone can find use for it, if they wish.

Estimation tools are often used in project management training and university courses. The models in these tools provide a broad view of the many inter-dependent influences on a project and this provides a useful start-point on which people can build a broader understanding of projects.

As well as learning, estimation models can reinforce people's confidence. At the start of a project, there are often a lot of vague statements and large commitments. Commercial estimation tools based on a wide range of industrial experiences, can provide a good second opinion of what the project should cost, if someone else was doing it.

In some sectors of industry, software development companies use cost models to guess at each other's costs and methods. For example, if you loose a contract to a competitor, use a model to see what assumptions they made to get the price. In similar way, major clients often use a set of different cost models to evaluate the feasibility of submitted tenders.

Many projects involve a high level of change requests after the project was budgeted. Some of these changes can be very important, which result in projects where the developers under-budget for the original tender then over-charge for changes. A more mature approach is to agree on a rate for any changes and write it into the contract. Cost models are particularly useful when they have been calibrated on a range of companies, because this provides a fair framework that describes the relative cost of changes from different size, product and project characteristics.

Some estimation tools will provide estimates for each component in the project, and for the typical phases and activities within these projects. Statistical and analogy-based methods can also be used to provide estimates for individual component phases based on other similar components. Provided the estimates are seen as achievable, they form a basis for planning. The availability of staff can be compared to requirements, and deviations can be monitored. The lack of precise estimation now becomes a matter for improved risk management.

### 4.3.3   The Word "Risk"

There are cultural variations across Europe in what is meant by "a risk" is used. Sometimes, it refers to the events (including good events), sometimes to the probability of the event occurring and sometimes to the impact or risk exposure.

We use "risk factor" for the event or uncertainty but other variations include risk item, risk driver, hazard, potential event and (just) risk.

We only use "risk" to describe the total risk exposure to the project objectives.

### 4.3.4   Can't Estimate? Then Manage the Risk

Every estimate that is based on previous projects, includes assumptions that problems will continue to occur in projects and cost as much as in previous projects.

Problems in projects are inevitable when new challenges are taken. Ideally the problems should occur because we are learning to do new things, but inevitably some also occur because we have failed to learn.

Within a project, every problem that occurs was once a risk factor, although no-one may have anticipated it. As a risk factor, there was a possibility it would occur, but once the possibility became a certainty then the risk factor became a problem or disaster. Part of risk management usually involves keeping a register of these risk factors. (An alternative approach, involving sensitivity analysis, is explained in the box at the end of this section.)

While estimates assume that some risk factors will occur as problems, the estimates also include the assumption that potential disasters and catastrophes will not occur. These are events that, if they occurred, would result in a dramatic increase in cost, causing failure of the project and perhaps even failure of the company.

Risk management typically involves a set of related activities, for which estimation methods can help. The examples shown below correspond to the model of risk management illustrated in Figure 4.6.

- Focussing the effort of risk assessment and management process requires a quick indication of the risk exposure to the project and hence an indication of how much effort should be allocated to the process of risk assessment and management. Cost models can help. By taking pessimistic views of project data, cost models can be used to predict worst case scenarios, and these can be compared to the expected outcome.
- Identification of risk factors is aided by a variety of techniques, among which is the identification of assumptions in key documents, such as plans, contracts, designs, and (significantly) the estimates on which plans are based.
- Assessing the size of risk factors involves the estimation of the likely impact of risks (in terms of cost, schedule, etc). Cost models can be used to provide simple "what-if" estimates, and analogy-based estimates can indicate the size of special cases which have happened before. Skilled users of cost models also find ways of using them to estimate the probability of risk factors.
- Planning the responses for risk factors has three steps. The first is to identify different types of response for each risk factor in turn. Cost models can be used to indicate combinations of project attributes that are likely to be difficult to achieve. The second step of planning a risk response is to estimate their cost and likely benefits. "What-if" estimates using estimation models and analogies

can sometimes be used to provide these estimates. The third step, is to find a sponsor.

- Changing the project to reduce risk factors includes modification to plans and designs. This will require new estimates.
- Research is often needed for risk factors that are so vague that they can not be analysed or their causes and influences are not sufficiently well understood for an effective risk response to be planned.
- Writing risk reports involves reporting on all the above. It can include reports on new estimates of the project cost and duration.

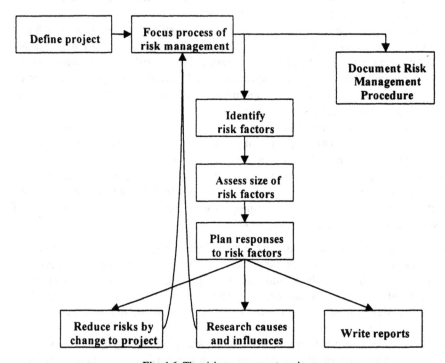

**Fig. 4.6** The risk management cycle.
Adapted from Project Risk Analysis and Management Guide, Ed. Peter Simon, David Hillson and Ken Newland. Published by the Association of Project Managers, 1997.

### 4.3.5   Risk Management Based on Sensitivity Models

Instead of managing potential problems and disasters (or as well as it), some risk managers prefer to use sensitivity analysis. This works in a different way.

First, a detailed project plan is needed, using a tool such as MS-Project.

Next, the week assumptions need to be identified within the project plan. Typically these relate to effort and duration of tasks.

Then, for each weak assumption, its likely behaviour has to be described by selecting a probability distribution and choosing its shape and size.

A commercial sensitivity analysis tool is needed to perform thousands of different variants of how the project may perform. It uses these to build a probability distributions of what may actually happen.

Finally, look for the tasks that most often correspond to delays. Look for ways of restructuring the project or changing resource allocation to improve this.

### 4.3.6   Worst Practice

Most of the so-called estimates people make are wrong, not because of fundamentally weak estimation models or methods, but because of mistakes. So as a prelude to understanding best practice, it helps to look first at some common examples of worst practice.

To start with, there are three common mistakes made at the strategic level:

- **Price-to-win.** Presenting a number as an estimate, when there is not enough information to make any kind of estimate. (For example, using guessed data within an estimation model results in a meaningless "estimate".) The correct strategy is to abandon the estimate and use risk management methods to learn more about the project before (later) making estimates.
- **Fantasies.** Some estimates are substantially influenced by a desire for cheapness. This is wrong – an estimate is a prediction of what will happen. The price quoted to clients may be entirely different to the estimate.
- **Padding.** Some estimates are secretly inflated knowing that work will expand to fill the extra time, and thus prove the estimator to be correct. This is very common when task leaders are asked to provide estimates of how long a task will take. If this is not corrected, the result is that such projects may be costed too high, and the work will expand to fill the time available.

Those mistakes are just the start. Even if they are avoided, there are still others that can be made, most noticeably with the choice and use of estimation methods.

- **Wrong methods.** It is a mistake to use an estimation method or model outside of the context for which it was designed. Especially, cost models are typically designed for particular types of project, however the increasing diversity of software development practices makes it increasingly difficult to model costs. (For example, even when calibrated with modern data, COCOMO-81 can no longer make realistic estimates for modern companies. Currently it is especially difficult to estimate for projects that make extensive use of Rapid Application Development or rely heavily on customising off-the-shelf software.

- **Inconsistent projects.** Estimates that are based on statistical analysis of a set of previous projects will only provide reliable estimates if there is consistency in the project procedures. Likewise, commercial cost estimation tools are only applicable if there were projects like yours is their database.
- **Calculation errors.** Estimates made using calculators and spreadsheets frequently have data entry, arithmetic and logical errors, especially when they have been developed over several iterations.

However some of the biggest mistakes in estimates, come from the data that is used.

- **Vague counting rules.** Much of the data used within estimates uses metrics that have vague instructions for how to make the measurement, and when. The metrics become subjective, and the result is great inconsistencies between different people.
- **Guessed data.** Using guesses introduces more errors. Especially, cost models that use the number of lines of code may be useful at explaining how much a completed project should have cost, but until the code has been written, there are problems. Instead it is better to use early-lifecycle measures, such as object-oriented metrics, or even counts of menu commands and database entities.
- **Aggregate data.** Combining different types of measurement into a single measure involves assumptions. For example, the complexity weightings used in function point counts, remain the same as they were in 1981, but our ability to handle complexity has changed.

Underlying these faults is the basic principle that, in estimates, errors accumulate. For example, errors in estimation methods are made worse by errors in data, and these may be further exaggerated by false strategies. There is a simple message to remember:

*Two Wrongs do not make a Right.*

More specifically, to make good estimates, concentrate on reducing every possible source of error.

### 4.3.7  Why are Function Points so Popular?

Function Points are based on raw data that is aggregated using a fixed set of constants. The inconsistencies between the people who count the values can be as much as ±50%, although people certified by the International Function Point User's Group tend to have much better consistency. The effort to count function points can vary from 2% to 6% of project costs. So why do so many people use function points?

Contracts between software developer and client need to specify the costs of adding late functional changes to the software. This requires a measure that combines both size and complexity, and which represents some kind of standard. The sums of money involved in changes are so large that it can fully justify the cost of measuring function points.

- Project managers frequently demand a simple answer to the question, "how big is it?" ... Function points give a single number, which is much easier to grasp than alternatives which give a whole set of numbers.
- There is a large industry and community behind Function Point Analysis. It is easy to get expert help, to find tools, conferences and trained staff. ... The problems of using function points are less than the intellectually superior alternatives.
- Function points provide a benchmark. They do not change with the years, they are not effected by different development processes or even different kinds of software. (With the development of Full Function Points, they now also cover real-time systems.) ... Function points are often the only way of making comparisons between companies.

### 4.3.8 Guidelines for Best Practice

Merely avoiding the mistakes above does not imply good practices are being used. The guidelines below indicate a set of good practices that are achievable, with effort. Best practice is common to every organisation that achieves a basic level of self-discipline and repeatability, although not necessarily that of ISO 9001 or CMM level 2. Some people and organisations will go further, working towards "ideal practice", however each will have its own ideal according to its own evolution.

A basic minimum for estimation includes:

- *Use 3 different estimates for any new project.* These should be produced by different people, or with different strategies and with different assumptions. At least one of the estimation methods should be analogy-based or calibrated using local project data. Compare the results, explain the differences and hence identify weaknesses in the estimates. If necessary, revise the estimates.
- *Keep a private record of how each estimate is made.* Later, refer back to these notes in order to see how to make better estimates.
- Make a new estimate following each major milestone in the project, using the information that is now available.

Use of competent estimation practices is just the start. It will remain difficult to achieve effective estimation if there is no pattern to the way projects are organised. If the organisation is not compliant with ISO 9001 or CMM Level 2, then the following issues of **process identification** also need to be addressed:

- For each type of activity or task in a project, provide a brief description of what it normally includes. Update the descriptions when more information becomes available. (As well as benefiting estimation, these descriptions are immediately useful for training and progress monitoring.)

- Use the task and activities to identify unorthodox features of new projects. These will indicate risks and areas that require special attention for estimation.
- Establish a rigorous definition of milestones as precise points in time corresponding to formal completion of documents, code, etc. (The point of picking points of this kind, is to avoid confused timing when one activity start major work while the previous activity is still active.)

All progress in improved estimation will become dependent on the availability of data. A good procedure is critically important for data collection.

- Examine how effort is tracked within projects. (Timesheets may not show unpaid overtime. They may also not allocate effort to the correct activity.) Without precise and concise effort recording the estimates will never be accurate.
- Establish which simple measures of size are available, and can be measured consistently. Especially look for measures of size that are available early in the lifecycle and have a strong statistical correlation to the effort of tasks or the duration of phases.
- Establish a database or spreadsheet to record data about projects.
- For every item of data that is to be collected, reduce its subjectivity by using a rigorous definition of how and when it is to be measured and recorded.

The integration with **risk management** is also very important. In particular:

- Create a risk register, listing the main risk factors to the project. Provide a short sentence of description for each, and guess at its likely impact and the probability that it will happen.
- Create an action list of how to improve the worst risk factors, and monitor who is doing what.
- Within each project, identify those risk factors which would have disastrous or catastrophic impact, and which the estimate assumes will not happen.

These represent guidelines to best practice, however they do not explain how to get to there, from here, and make the changes last. This is described in the next section.

### 4.3.9   Making it Last

Organisations depend heavily on the repeatable process that indicates what people should do, and when. Whether the procedures are written or merely implied by precedent, they help people co-ordinate their activities and learn how to contribute. Improved practice at estimation and related activities must become part of these repeatable procedures.

There have been many attempts to improve practices of data collection, estimation and risk management. Frequently they fail. They fail, not because the tools are wrong, or the training inadequate, but because a key issue has not been considered. In particular, there are things that are frequently forgotten:

- **Lack of integration,** such that the new methods are expected to stand alone, often without adaptation to fit with other procedures.
- **Lack of experience,** where staff are taught the principles of a new method, but given too little opportunity to try the ideas and exchange experiences with other people.
- **Lack of a stepwise progress plan,** where people try to introduce too much change, too quickly.
- **Too abstract,** where the new methods can not be easily applied because they require creative and laborious interpretation.
- **Lack of positive feedback,** where the new methods give no benefit or feedback to key players, and consequently there is little reason for them to help.
- **Wrong vision,** where the new methods imply the wrong priorities for the company. (Some organisations are driven for continual process improvement, others by a need for market and technical mastery, and still others by a short-term instinct for survival.)

All of these mistakes are avoidable, but they need careful attention. One significant contribution is the commitment of key individuals, and especially the individuals in each company who are first to use the new methods, and consequently provide leadership to others.

### 4.3.10  Personal Objectives

However good the training and tools, estimation will always be limited by the dedication and professionalism of the people who perform the estimation process. So by way of conclusion to these Guidelines, we propose a Code Of Conduct to which estimators should aspire.

### 4.3.11  Code of Conduct for Professional Estimators

From this day forward, I do solemnly promise to regard myself as a Professional Estimator only when, to the best my abilities within the constraints imposed upon me, I fulfil the following code of conduct.

My reports will, …
- be clear, relevant and appropriate,
- be delivered on time,
- include honest predictions of the future, and
- will not never present a target as an estimate.

When estimating, ...

- I will seek to understand the nature of the project and not reply solely on data supplied by other people,
- I will not rely on data with vague or unusable counting rules, and
- I will consider, list any major risks that it is assumed will not occur.

I will seek continuously to improve, ...

- by comparing the project results to my original estimates,
- by keeping notes of how I made the estimate, and later use these to learn how I could do better next time, and
- by seeking to extend my knowledge by reading and by exchange of experience with other professionals.

I will seek to compare Like with Like, comparing, ...

- companies against similar companies,
- tasks against similar tasks,
- technology against similar technology, and
- new data against data taken from the same phase of previous projects.

As I achieve expertise, ...

- I will exchange my experience with other practitioners,
- I will seek to teach my colleagues, and
- I will build the structures for my successors to continue the progress that I have made.

# 5 Resources for Practitioners

O. Bécart
Editions HIGHWARE

## 5.1 Methods and Tools

There are many methods and tools designed to support estimation of software projects, to manage projects and/or the project lifecycle. Many of them are adapted to particular kinds of software (real time software, databases, object oriented software, user interface development, and so on).

In the following sections, we list and briefly describe some of these methods and tools. We encourage the reader to continuously evaluate the tools and methods available because improvements and new offerings are always being made available.

### 5.1.1 Fusion

Fusion is a systematic software development method for object-oriented software that was developed at Hewlett-Packard Laboratories in Bristol, England. The method integrates and extends the best features of earlier methods, including OMT, Booch and CRC. Fusion is a full-coverage method, providing a direct route from a requirements definition through analysis and design to a programming language implementation.

### 5.1.2 Vision Based Methodology™

The VBM Methodology for Systems Development was developed by ITMWeb Media Technology. Russ Finney wrote the following overview of the methodology.

#### Activity 1: Selling the Idea
A project idea doesn't go anywhere unless it actually becomes a project. This VBM activity examines various approaches to building a base of support for a proposed effort, and then actually winning the necessary approval and financing.

### Activity 2: Creating the Plan
Before the project effort gets underway, the plan should be completely thought through. As a part of this, staffing requirements should be determined, high level goals and calendar milestones should be charted, and development activities should be outlined. This VBM activity focuses on the planning process and its use throughout the life of the project.

### Activity 3: Building the Team
Determining who will be on the team is one thing, but keeping the team together and performing at its maximum potential is another. This VBM activity explores a multitude of team building and project management approaches, and their effective use throughout the systems development effort.

### Activity 4: Uncovering the Requirements
A critical step in the system development/enhancement process is the definition of the project requirements in business client terminology. This VBM activity examines an assortment of requirements gathering techniques, with a strong emphasis on the utilisation of a facilitated session approach for collection and confirmation of the bulk of the major system functional definition.

### Activity 5: Modelling the Business
As the business requirements are being collected, a "picture" of the important business information and the related processes begins to emerge. Capturing this evolving image in a manner which serves as a communication tool for both the technical as well as the business project participants, is the centrepiece of this VBM activity. An overview is provided of many of today's current major modelling techniques.

### Activity 6: Conceptualising the System
Turning business requirements into business solutions is the act of defining how the requirements will be satisfied, which technological platforms will be utilised, and what the system will look like. This VBM activity reviews the transformation of logical requirements into physical components. In addition, the discussion highlights current software development standards and technological trends.

### Activity 7: Creating the Vision
Designing the business components of the system, and then putting this vision into a form which can be reviewed by the business clients, is the focus of this VBM activity. Strong emphasis is placed on the use of an iterative prototyping approach for the design of the various screen, form, window, and report layouts.

### Activity 8: Specifying the Vision

Each individual system component should be carefully defined, and its internal workings should be clearly documented, in the form of a program specification. This VBM activity outlines various specification approaches which can be employed to capture the functional details based on the contemplated construction methodology. Special attention is paid to traditional procedural programming, automated code generation, and object-oriented programming.

### Activity 9: Constructing the System

No matter which methodological route is taken, at some point someone will have to either generate the program logic or bear down and write the actual program code. This VBM activity takes an extensive look at all of the considerations and techniques which surround this activity. A sharp focus is aimed at the key process of turning specifications into fully integrated and tested programs.

### Activity 10: Reselling the Idea

Once the system has been completed, it must be introduced into the business environment. This VBM activity examines the issues and approaches involved with managing the organisational change process, guiding the system through acceptance testing, and equipping the business clients with the training and documentation they will require to gain their independence from the system builders!

More on this method can be found on the site of the company ITMWeb: http://www.itmweb.com/method.htm

## 5.1.3  Application Development Methodology[11]

The Application Development Methodology provides a standard consistent way of developing and maintaining information systems. It provides uniform technology and expectations for all project participants. The consistency reduces the learning curve when bringing new people into an on-going project. It also serves as a roadmap for both experienced and inexperienced staff.

To do this, ADM defines precisely the activities and their deliverables, and the roles and responsibilities of the participants of the project.

Different paths are proposed by this methodology for :

- for feasibility /assessment projects
- for small system projects
- for large systems projects
- for purchased system projects

---

[11] University of California, Davis

- for RAPID application projects
- for Business Process Reengineering projects (BPR)

The advantage of this methodology is to be independent of any tool.

More on this subject can be found on the site of University of California Davis : http://sysdev.ucdavis.edu/WEBADM/

### 5.1.4   Silverrun

Applied Information Science, a Californian Corporation, did test the 1997 version of the case tools of Silverrun.
The following report has been written after the test :

*"Silverrun* is a large and deep set of tools for database modelling and engineering. At the moment *Silverrun* is perhaps uniquely positioned among CASE tools.
*Silverrun* integrates the three classic fundamental data design components based on a common presentation approach and shared design definitions:

- Discovery of requirements, definitions, and structures via data flow diagramming in the **BPM** module (which we did not review)
- Conceptual modelling via Chen style Entity-Relationship diagrams in the **ERX** module (screen shot above on the left)
- Advanced relational schema design and DDL generation in the **RDM** module (screen shot above on the right)

Each of these three modules is a separate product, licensed per seat. Since the per module cost is about the same as the total cost of *PowerDesigner* or *ERwin*, *Silverrun* can be somewhat more expensive, depending on configuration and user population. Nonetheless the cost difference alone is moderate and hardly a deterrent to enterprise scale users who may desire *Silverrun*'s benefits.
In addition, an optional Enterprise version of *Silverrun* (**RDM** only to date) joins the big leagues by working directly over a relational database dictionary. Standard versions capture a model snapshot in a proprietary file local to the user. A product facility is provided to manage the reconciliation of multiple models. The Enterprise version, on the other hand, displays each object live from its shared RDBMS dictionary (in Oracle, Sybase, ...), which handles locking, updates, and global refresh at the object level.
Based on its solid foundation in methodology, depth of features, and modular integration, we would be tempted to rate *Silverrun* as a strong leader in the CASE data modelling field. Yet we cannot because all of us participating in this review had the same overall impression: *Silverrun*'s style is bulky, clumsy, and slow to the point that it inhibits, rather than enables, design inspiration.
We constantly felt as if we were dragging a load of discarded library books through knee-deep melting snow. Menus are very long and intimidating with un-

obvious choices. Tool pallets contain overlapping and confusing icons. Accessing graphic objects requires knowledge of specific tool behaviours. "Connectors" are defined separately from "Directions". A number of its internal rules are only enforced by batch procedures, rather than as real-time validations. Throughout *Silverrun* understanding is encumbered by extensive jargon unknown in the standard lexicon of data modelling.

At a more general level, we found the methodology framework imposed by *Silverrun*'s **ERX** module to be out of date and incomplete. The Chen style Entity-Relationship modelling in the **ERX** module forces the dated notion of "relationships" as objects separate and distinct from entities – a concept which has been discarded by most practitioners in favour of the more streamlined and understandable Information Engineering technique.

*Silverrun* falls far short of PowerDesigner in the level of abstraction which one can employ in conceptual and physical modelling. *Silverrun*'s sub-typing is implemented only at the physical level (**RDM** "Choices") and offers no flexibility in mapping conceptual sub-types into normalised or denormalised tables. Candidate keys are not supported, although their common weak side effect of "alternate keys" are. There is no facility in the **ERX** module to model purely conceptual entities which externalise an attribute definition without generating a table. Several other deficiencies reinforce our opinion of *Silverrun*'s weak abstraction.

These unacceptable flaws in a basically strong product are very disappointing to us. *Silverrun* provides multi-platform desktop support, excellent on-line help, extensive printed documentation, good user support policies, and, in our limited experience, robust, reliable code that performs well. If you do not share our rather strong and personal opinions on modelling style and abstraction, if you cannot work on Windows, or if you must have true interactive multi-user data modelling, then seriously consider *Silverrun*."

End of the report.

## 5.1.5 The Booch Method

The Booch method covers the analysis and design phases of an OO-system. Booch sometimes is criticised for his big set of different symbols. It's true that Booch defines a lot of symbols to document almost every design decision. If you work with this method, you notice that you will never use all these symbols and diagrams. You start with class and object diagrams in the analysis phase and refine these diagrams in various steps. Only when you are ready to generate code, you add some design symbols. And this is where Booch is strong: you can really document your OO-code.

The Models of Object-Oriented Analysis and Design support multiple, interrelated views of a system under development.

The Booch method defines different models to describe your system. The logical model (problem domain) is represented in the class- and object structure. In the class-diagram you construct the architecture, the static model. The object-diagram shows how the classes interact with each other, it captures some moments in the life of the system and helps you so to describe the dynamic behaviour.

The module and process architecture describes the physical allocation of the classes to modules and processes.

### Macro Process

- Establish core requirements (conceptualisation).
- Develop a model of the desired behaviour (analysis).
- Create an architecture (design).
- Evolve the implementation (evolution).
- Manage post delivery evolution (maintenance).

### Micro Process

- Identify the classes and objects at a given level of abstraction.
- Identify the semantics of these classes and objects.
- Identify the relationships among these classes and objects.
- Specify the interface and then the implementation of these classes and objects.

Booch supports the iterative and incremental development of a system.

### 5.1.6    Disco

DisCo (Distributed Co-operation) is a formal specification method for reactive systems. It incorporates a specification language, a methodology for developing specifications using the language, and tool support for the methodology. Currently the support tools include an animation facility for executing specifications, a tool for visualising execution histories as scenarios, and a link to a mechanical theorem prover for verification.

The method has a is solid formal basis, but the specification language uses concepts and notations familiar to people with a conventional software engineering background. To get a taste of DisCo see the distributed sort and other examples.

DisCo focuses on early verification and validation of behavioural properties. Emphasis is on collective behaviour, rather than on behaviour of individual objects. The joint action model of execution enables modelling of behaviour at a high level of abstraction. In particular, collective behaviour can be specified without fixing the interfaces of objects and without indicating which objects initiate communication.

More information is available on the site http://www.cs.tut.fi/laitos/DisCo/.

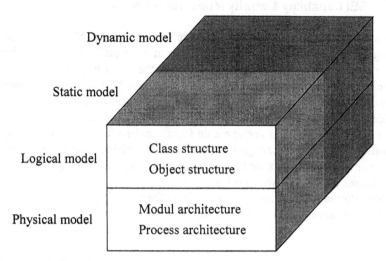

**Fig. 5.1** The Aspects of an Object-Oriented Structure Model

## 5.1.7 EROOS

EROOS, which stands for Entity-Relationship Object Oriented Specifications, is an object oriented software development method crafted by the Research Group on Software Development Methodology of the Department of Computer Science of the Katholieke Universiteit Leuven. A good introduction can be found in the EROOS Reference Manual v1.0. It reflects those parts of the method that are currently considered stable. Results of further research will be reflected in consecutive versions of this Reference Manual.

The EROOS method is the condensation of experiences with object-oriented software development. It features 3 phases: *Analysis, Design* and *Implementation*. With the method, formal yet ergonomic specifications are composed using interrelated basic building blocks which are highly reusable. The method provides in basic building blocks for each of the fundamental concepts used: *Objects and Classes, Relations, Attributes, Constraints and Triggers, Events* and *Queries*.

The EROOS Reference Manual v1.0 is only concerned with the analysis phase. It features 6 chapters: "I. Classes and Initial Functionality", "II. Relations and Refinement Functionality", "III. Attributes and Decoration Functionality", "IV. Constraints", "V. Generalisation / Specialisation" and "VI. Functionality". Each of these chapters explains the semantics, describes the textual and graphical syntax of the EROOS concept in question, and shows how to use it and how not to use it.

The EROOS Research Group can be contacted through e-mail at: eroos_contact @cs.kuleuven.ac.be

Updated versions of this document will be available by ftp with URL ftp:// ftp.cs.kuleuven.ac.be/ftp/pub/EROOS/documentation/EROOS.Reference.Manual/.

### 5.1.8   SEI Capability Maturity Model for Software

The Capability Maturity Model for Software (CMM or SW-CMM) is a model for judging the maturity of the software processes of an organisation and for identifying the key practices that are required to increase the maturity of these processes.

The software community has developed the SW-CMM under the stewardship of the Software Engineering Institute (SEI). This model is one of the three that provide the basis for the initial CMM IntegrationSM (CMMISM) product suite.

The Software CMM has become a de facto standard for assessing and improving software processes. Through the SW-CMM, the SEI and community have put in place an effective means for modelling, defining, and measuring the maturity of the processes used by software professionals.

More information and links are available on the site
http://www.sei.cmu.edu/cmm/cmm.html.

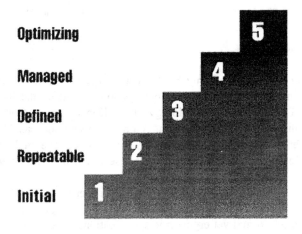

Fig. 5.2  The Maturity Levels of the SEI Model

### 5.1.9   Shlaer-Mellor Method

The Shlaer-Mellor Method provides comprehensive coverage for the analysis, design, and implementation phases of the software development lifecycle. This section briefly describes each of the major steps in the Shlaer-Mellor Method and its contribution to the development lifecycle. It characterises the activities in each step and introduces the fundamental concepts on which the activities are based.

In order to describe the Shlaer-Mellor process in detail, the process is broken down into the steps listed below. These steps distinguish between the work according to different types of domains, namely, the application domain, the service domains, and the architectural (translation) domain. These types of domains are described in the next section.

- Partition the system into domains.
- Analyse the application domain.
- Confirm the analysis through static verification and dynamic verification (simulation).
- Extract the requirements for the service domains.
- Analyse the service domains.
- Specify the components of the architectural domain.
- Build the architectural components.
- Translate the models of each domain using the architectural components

More information and links are available on the site
http://www.projtech.com/info/smmethod.html.

### 5.1.10 Process Engineering Methodology

The Process Engineering Methodology (PEM) defines a structured approach to process specification and automation.

The PEM is divided into two volumes. Volume 1 contains a group of papers related to the background and development of the methodology. Volume 2 is divided into two parts. Part 1 is the Process Engineering Software Process Guidebook. A guidebook is an instance of a process logical specification work product of the methodology. Part 2 illustrates process definition development step by step through the methodology. In addition, process related glossaries, product definitions, and references are separately accessible.

More information and links are available on the site
http://www.asset.com/Boeing/rde/pem/.

### 5.1.11 Unified Modelling Language

The Unified Modelling Language (UML) is the industry-standard language for specifying, visualising, constructing, and documenting the artefacts of software systems. It simplifies the complex process of software design, making a "blueprint" for construction. The UML definition was led by methodologists: Grady Booch, Ivar Jacobson, and Jim Rumbaugh.

More information and links are available on the site
http://www.rational.com/uml/ and
http://www.platinum.com/corp/uml/uml.htm.

### 5.1.12  Dynamic Systems Development Method (DSDM)

The Dynamic Systems Development Method (DSDM) is a framework of controls for the development of IT systems to tight timescales. It is independent of any particular set of tools and techniques and can be used with object-oriented and structured analysis and design approaches in environments ranging from the individual PC to global distributed systems. DSDM has been used successfully by organisations in both the public and private sectors.

The lifecycle which DSDM uses is iterative and incremental. This move away from the traditional, waterfall approach is possible because of the new technologies which enable visualisation of the interim products of system development. Indeed the move is essential if IT solution providers, whether internal IT departments or external suppliers, are to deliver working systems in the ever decreasing timescales demanded by businesses today. While the waterfall approach is necessary for many system developments, where a system is suitable for RAD and is required in a short timescale, the waterfall lifecycle is inappropriate. In waterfall projects, advantage can be gained from using components of the DSDM approach to reduce the time to delivery and to ensure that the right requirements are addressed.

More information and links are available on the site
http://www.dsdm.org/.

### 5.1.13  HOOD

HOOD is a method of hierarchical decomposition of the design into software units based on identification of objects, classes and operations reflecting problem domain entities or more abstract objects related to digital programming entities. It is intended for the Architectural Design, Detailed Design and coding for software to be developed in programming languages such as Ada, C, or FORTRAN, as well as in object oriented languages such as C++, Ada95 or Eiffel.

The HOOD method comprises textual and associated diagrammatic representations allowing formal refinement, automated checking, user customisable documentation generation and target language source code generation.

The HOOD method was developed in 1987 under European Space Agency (ESA) contract A0/1-1890/86/NL/MA by a consortium of CISI, CRI A/S and Matra Marconi Space. HOOD has been selected by ESA projects as the design method for the Architectural Design phase. Since, HOOD is being more and more selected by large, complex or long lived project from aerospace, defence and industry.

Since 1989 the HOOD Manuals have been developed, in response to user experience, by the HOOD Working Group comprising representatives of ESTEC, Columbus and Hermes projects and later under control by the HOOD User Group (HUG).

In 1991, the HUG was set-up as a non profit organisation aiming to provide support for sharing experience and to control the evolution of the method. The HUG is organised in a Steering Group (HSG) in charge of administrative issues, and in a Technical Group (HTG) in charge of all technical issues possibly delegating work to specific Working Groups. The HUG is based at:

C/O Spacebel Informatique
111 rue Colonel Bourg
B-1140 BRUSSELS
Belgium
Tel: +32.2.730.46.11
Fax: +32.2.726.85.13
e-mail: hug@spacebel.be

The HOOD Reference Manual Issue 3.1 was further developed in 1991 by the HOOD Technical Group and approved for two years by vote by the HOOD User Group at the Pisa (Italy) April 3rd 1992 HUG meeting. The present document HOOD Reference Manual Release 4 (ftp.estec.esa.nl/ pub/wm/wme/HOOD/ HOOD_Ref_Manual_4) was further developed in 1994 by the HOOD Technical Group and approved for two years by vote by the HOOD User Group at the London (UK) HUG meeting in February 1995. Initially developed for Ada83 program developments, HOOD is now targeting Ada95 as well as more classical and object oriented languages and systems. HOOD puts the emphasis on interface and behaviour definition and mastering, some issues that were rather neglected by other design methods. Moreover HOOD appears more and more as the framework for mastering and integration of the development of software components which may be developed with different target language and technologies (MMI generators, DBMS interface generators, rule system and KBS generators). HOOD is thus supporting complex programming and development in the large, relying on code generator technology from high level and when possible, formal notations. As a result HOOD fills primarily the needs of prime contractors and integrators. Providing a standard inter-change format, the HOOD method addresses also pragmatic reuse, tool inter-operability and design perennially. HOOD is thus the method of choice for large, long-lived projects where reuse, reliability and maintainability are key issues.

### 5.1.14 Et Cetera...

We recommend to practitioners to update these searches on the web with the key words "software development tools" or "software project management tools" plus some keywords linked to their own domain.

A glance at http://www.methodology.org/ gives also information on the subject.

## 5.2   Books

Several key contributors to this book made some recommendations for further readings. These are listed here.

### 5.2.1   Cost Models for Future Software Life Cycle Processes: COCOMO 2.0

Boehm B., Clark B., Horowitz E., Westland C., Madachy R., Selby R.: "Cost models for future software life cycle processes: COCOMO 2.0". Annals of Software Engineering Special Volume on Software Process and Product Measurement, 1995,

### 5.2.2   Opportunity-Driven Control of Quality and Cost

Adrian Cowderoy, Mario Bucolo and Fred Schindler: "Opportunity-driven control of quality and cost." Project Control for Software Quality, Shaker Publishing, ISBN 90-423-0075-2.

### 5.2.3   Function Points Counting Practices Manual

"Function Points Counting Practices Manual – Release 4.0", International Function Point Users Group (IFPUG), Westerville, Ohio, USA, January 1994.

### 5.2.4   Managing Risk: Methods for Software Systems Development

Elaine M. Hall, Managing Risk. Methods for Software Systems Development. Addison Wesley, 1998. ISBN 0-201-25592-8.

### 5.2.5   On the Compatibility between Full Function Points and IFPUG Function Points

Serge Oligny and Alain Abran: "On the compatibility between Full Function Points and IFPUG function points." Project Control for Software Quality, Shaker Publishing, ISBN 90-423-0075-2.

### 5.2.6 Project Risk Analysis and Management Guide

Peter Simon, David Hillson and Ken Newland (Ed.): Project Risk Analysis and Management Guide, Association of Project Managers, 1997, ISBN 0 9531590 0 0.

### 5.2.7 Earned Value Project Management

Fleming, Quentin W. / Koppelman, Joel M. : Earned Value Project Management ISBN:1880410389 , Jan 1996

### 5.2.8 Software Project Cost & Schedule Estimating: Best Practices

Roetzheim, William H, / Beasley, Reyna : Software Project Cost & Schedule Estimating: Best Practices ISBN: 0136820891, November 1997

### 5.2.9 A Guide to the Project Management Body of Knowledge (PMBOK)

Duncan, William R. / PMI Standards Committee : A Guide to the Project Management Body of Knowledge (PMBOK) ISBN:1880410133 , Jan 96 , PJMI

### 5.2.10 Object-Oriented Analysis and Design with Applications

Grady Booch: Object-oriented Analysis and Design with Applications, 2nd edition. Benjamin Cummings, Redwood City. ISBN 0-8053-5340-2, 1993

### 5.2.11 Object-Oriented System Development

*Object-Oriented System Development* by Dennis de Champeaux, Douglas Lea, and Penelope Faure was published by Addison Wesley (www.awl.com), copyright © 1993 by Hewlett-Packard Company. (ISBN 0-201-56355-X).

Software systems are often components of general systems. This book discusses only object-oriented approaches to developing software systems. The roots of the OO paradigm include AI frames and programming languages including *Simula*.

The structured paradigm focuses on decomposing behaviours. The OO paradigm focuses on objects, classes, and inheritance. The two paradigms do not mix well. While the OO paradigm tightly integrates the development phases of analysis, design and implementation, intrinsic differences between these phases should not be blurred. OO methods are compatible with prototyping efforts, especially those constructed in order to elucidate otherwise unknown requirement fragments.

### 5.2.12  Modélisation Objet avec UML

"Modélisation objet avec UML" Book by Pierre-Alain Muller (pa.muller@ essaim.univ-mulhouse.fr)
ISBN: 2-212-08966-X
Editor: Eyrolles, 61 Bld Saint-Germain, 75240 Paris CEDEX.
420 pages, with CD that includes the English documentation UML 1.0, PDF reader, Rose 4.0 for evaluation and the model of the example presented in the book. It includes 5 chapters:

- the genesis of UML.
- the object-oriented approach.
- the UML notation.
- towards a development process.
- a case study.

Annexes about the transition from OMT and Booch to UML code generation examples (C++, JAVA, IDL, Visual Basic, SQL)

### 5.2.13  Software-Engineering: Objektorientierte Software-Entwicklung mit der Unified Modeling Language

Objektorientierte Software-Entwicklung mit der Unified Modeling Language
Springer-Verlag; Berlin, Heidelberg, New York, 1998, ISBN 3-540-63309-X

## 5.3  Organisations

### 5.3.1  International Project Management Association

International Project Management Association
P.O. Box 30, Monmouth NP5 4YZ, United Kingdom
Tel: 44 1594 531007; Fax: 44 1594 531008 Email: ipma@btinternet.com
    This association has local branches, for example :

### Portugal

President: Nuno Ponces de Carvalho
Associacao Portuguesa de Gestao de Projectos (APOGEP)
Av. Almirante Reis No 127-1-dto
1150 Lisboa

PORTUGAL
Tel: + 351 1 314 5787
Fax: + 351 1 357 0410
Email: apogep@mail.telepac.pt

## Spain

Chairman: Prof. Juan Luis Cano Fernandez
Asociacion Espanola de Ingenieria de Proyectos (AEIPRO)
Centro Politecnico Superior de Ingenieros
C/Maria de Luna 3
50015 Zaragoza
SPAIN
Tel: + 34 976 76 1910
Fax: + 34 976 76 1861
Email: jlcano@posta.unizar.es
Web: http://www.cps.unizar.es/~aeipro

## Sweden

Chair: Catarina Meland
Svenskt ProjektForum
Box 830
S-111 36 Stockholm
Phone: +46 8 22 14 13
Fax: + 46 8 22 14 13
Email: info@projforum.se
Web: http://www.projforum.se

## United Kingdom

Chairman: Don Heath
The Association for Project Management
150 West Wycombe Road
HIGH WYCOMBE
Bucks HP12 3AE
UNITED KINGDOM
Tel: + 44 1494 440 090
Fax: + 44 1494 528 937
Email: secretariat@apm-UK.demon.co.uk
Web: http://www.apm.org.uk

## 5.3.2    Project Management Institute

Project Management Institute
4 Campus Boulevard
Newtown Square, PA 19073-3299 USA
Phone: 610/356-4600
Fax: 610/356-4647
E-Mail: pmihq@pmi.org
    These associations have local branches. Many of them have a web site, a re-
search on the web with key words "project management associations" gives a lot
of results and everybody is able to find an association in his country and / or his
domain. For example in the United Kingdom you may find 5.3.3.

## 5.3.3    Association for Project Management

The Association for Project Management is the United Kingdom based organisation dedicated to advancing the science of Project Management and the professional development of Project Managers and Project Management Specialists. It
was formed in 1972 to advance the discipline of Project Management and to promote the professional development of Project Managers in all business areas.

Mrs Doreen Bevan
105 West Wycombe Road, High Wycombe HP12 3AE
E-mail: secretariat@apm-uk.demon.co.uk

## 5.3.4    International Cost Engineering Council

The International Cost Engineering Council (ICEC) is an non-political and non-
profit organisation which was founded in 1976 with the object of promoting co-
operation between national and multinational cost engineering, quantity surveying
and project management organisations world-wide for their mutual well being and
that of their individual members. ICEC member societies are located in more than
30 countries, and have chapters or sections in many additional countries. Through
these chapters and sections, ICEC has access to more than 50,000 cost engineers
and project managers in over 120 different nations. Regular ICEC meetings are
attended by delegates of the member societies where subjects of common interests
are exchanged and discussed. Each member society has one vote on the Council.
    This association has local branches, for example :

Association Francophone de Management de Projet (AFITEP)
(French-speaking Project Management Association)
ICEC Member, 1982
17 rue de Turbigo

F-75002 Paris
FRANCE
E mail: info@afitep.fr
ICEC delegate: Bernard Beudet, afitep@easynet.fr
http://www.afitep.fr

Projektiyhdistys (PRY)
(Project Management Association of Finland – PMAF)
ICEC Member 1980
PO Box 132
FIN 02101 Espoo
FINLAND
E-mail: pty@innopoli.fi
Executive Officer: Rauno Puskala, rauno.puskala@synertek.fi
ICEC delegate: Eero Linkama, eero.linkama@poyry.fi

Foreningen for Dansk Projektledelse (FDP)
(Project Management Association of Denmark)
ICEC Member, 1993
Saettedammen 4
DK 3400 Hillerod
DENMARK
E mail: info@projektforeningen.dk
http://www.projektforeningen.dk
ICEC delegate: Soeren Christensen, sc@rdg.bane.dk
Alternate Delegate: Hans Tørskeff, ht@htms.dk

Associazione Italiana di Ingegneria Economica (AICE)
(Italian Association of Total Cost Management)
ICEC Member, 1980
Via D.Cimarosa 17
I-20144 Milano
ITALY
ICEC delegate: Gianluca de Castri, gdicastri@uli.it

The AICE started its activity in 1979 and, from then, is working in strict co-operation with the Bocconi University in Milano, where seminars and workshops are organised, on a regular basis, in order to discuss selected topics of cost management and related disciplines. The AICE also co-operates also with the University of Genova, Faculty of Architecture, the University of Torino, Faculty of Economics and the Polytechnic of Milano, Faculty of Engineering, as well as with other professional societies.

The magazine Ingegneria Economica is published on a quarterly basis; it is mainly in the Italian language, although some text can be in English.

Every year a National Forum is held at Bocconi University. The official language is Italian but papers in other European languages are accepted.

### 5.3.5   HOOD User Group

The HOOD User Group – HUG – is a non profit organisation registered in Belgium.

Its main purpose is to secure the maintenance of the HOOD – Hierarchical Object Oriented Design – method. It is further a forum for the discussion and exchange of experience concerning the use of HOOD and other related methods and procedures.

The HOOD method was originally defined under a contract for the European Space Agency – ESA – and was executed by CISI, MATRA and CRI. Since then the method has been considerably enhanced and several tools are available on the market in support of the method. Apart from having been the preferred design method in many ESA projects it has also been used in several non-ESA projects, in particular in projects related to ADA and C++.

Typical HUG members are users of the method, including representatives from industry, organisations (e.g. ESA) and universities, and tool vendors. The membership may be paid by a company or an organisation but must at any time be associated to a particular person which may be represented by others only under certain conditions.

The issue of new versions of the Hood Reference Manual – HRM – is under the full responsibility of the HUG. New versions can only be released based on voting by the HUG assembly involving members with voting right. The HRM issue 3.1.1 may be purchased from Masson, France or Prentice Hall, UK. The HOOD 4 version is going to be delivered soon to all the members and should be submitted to vote in October 95.

The HUG will meet at least once a year. It elects the following permanent administrative and technical groups:

- HOOD Steering Group – HSG – is the governing administrative assembly between HUG meetings. It consists of 6 people out of which 5 are elected directly from the HUG. The vice chairman of the HSG is the chairman of the HTG. The chairman and the treasurer form the HOOD Administrative Group.
- HOOD Technical Group – HTG – which is a technical group of 12 people elected from the HUG assembly. It is responsible for the generation of HRM updates and the issue of technical reports and letters relevant to the use of HOOD. The screening and handling of HRM problem reports originating from members of HUG is a major activity of the HTG. The HTG also issues the HOOD News. The HTG chairman is the vice chairman of the HSG. Additional working groups may be associated to the HTG.

- HOOD Administrative Group – HAG – consists of the HSG chairman and the treasurer and is responsible for the daily administration, including the HUG finances which are managed via co-signature of the Chairman and the Treasurer.

Half of all members of the administrative and technical groups must make their positions available for re-election each year.

The membership fees of the HUG are used to cover some of the expenses occurring in connection with some of the administrative and technical work performed within and for the HTG and HAG.

Several types of memberships are available. Members will automatically receive the HRM updates, the HOOD News and other technical information available from the HUG. Members may enter articles into the HOOD News.

## 5.4  Important Conferences

- QAOOSE2000 4th Int. ECOOP Workshop Quantitative Approaches Object-Oriented Software Engineering; 2000 June 13; Cannes, France; OO Metrics; deadline for papers 2000 March 24. (2000-03-08)
- EASE 2000 4th Int. Conf. Empirical Assessment and Evaluation in Software Engineering; 2000 April 17-19; Staffordshire, UK; *Software Measurement, Process Assessment*; program available. (http://www.keele.ac.uk/depts/cs/ease/)
- ESCOM-SCOPE 2000 11th European Software Control and Metrics Conf., 3rd Software Certification Programme in Europe; 2000 April 18-20; Munich, Germany; *Software Measurement, Quality Improvement*; program available. (http://www.escom.co.uk/escom/)
- ICSE 2000 22nd Int. Conf. Software Engineering: 2000 June 04-11; Limerick, Ireland; *Software Engineering, Empirical Studies, Process Improvement*; program available. (http://www.ul.ie/~icse2000/)
- ESEPG 2000 5th European Software Engineering Process Group Conf.; 2000 June 05-08; Amsterdam, Netherlands; *Process Improvement*; deadline for proposals 2000 January 14/28.
- ICSE 2000 Workshop Multidisciplinary Approaches in Empirical Software Engineering Research; 2000 June 05; Limerick, Ireland; *Empirical Research*; submission deadline 2000 February 25. (http://www.csr.uvic.ca/icse2000/)
- TOOLS Europe 2000 Technology Object-Oriented Languages Systems; 2000 June 05-08; Mont Saint-Michel/St-Malo, France; *Object-Orientation, OO Metrics*; paper deadline 2000 January 31. (http://www.irisa.fr/TE2000/)
- ECOOP 2000 14th European Conf. Object-Oriented Programming; 2000 June 12-16; Cannes, France; *OO Metrics*; program available. (ecoop2000.unice.fr/)
- QAOOSE2000 4th Int. ECOOP Workshop Quantitative Approaches Object-Oriented Software Engineering; 2000 June 13; Cannes, France; *OO Metrics*; deadline for papers 2000 March 24. (http://www.iro.umontreal.ca/~sahraouh/qaoose/)

- PROFES 2000 Int. Conf. Product Focused Software Process Improvement; 2000 June 20-22; Oulu, Finland; *Process Improvement, Software Measurement*; paper deadline 2000 January 31. (http://www.ele.vtt.fi/profes2000/)
- INSPIRE 2000 5th Int. Conf. Software Process Improvement; 2000 September 06-08; Nicosia, Cyprus; *Process Improvement, Software Quality*; paper deadline 2000 April 30. (idun.unl.ac.uk/~11georgiadou/inspire2000/)
- IFPUG 2000 Ann. Conf.; 2000 September 11-15; San Diego, California, USA; *Function Point Analysis, Software Measurement*; submission deadline 2000 March 15 (http://www.ifpug.org/home/docs/presentations.html)
- CONQUEST 2000 Conf. Quality Engineering Software Technology; 2000 September 14-15; Franken, Germany; *Software Quality*; paper deadline 2000 April 14. (http://www.asqf.de/english/conquest/frm_conq.htm)
- ESCOM 2001 12th Europ. Software Control Metrics Conf.; 2001 April 02-06; London, UK; *Software Measurement*; abstract deadline 2000 September 15. (http://www.mmhq.co.uk/2001/escom/index.shtml)
- METRICS 2001 7th Int. Software Metrics Symposium; 2001 April 04-06; London, UK; *Software Measurement*; abstract deadline 2000 July 15. (http://www.mmhq.co.uk/2001/metrics/index.shtml)

World-wide conferences and events re announced on:
http://www.esi.es/WorldwideEvents/

## 5.5    Web Sites

### *http://www.cs.uidaho.edu/~billjunk/courses/cs482/weblinks.html*
This web site from the University of Idaho contains an index that provides access to a number of other important web sites.
Sections include:
- Consulting Organisations
- Education & Training
- Links to Other Resources
- Original Material
- Project Management Tools
- Management
- Software Measurement
- Software Process
- Software Project Management

### *http://sunset.usc.edu/COCOMOII/*
Update of the continuing research efforts on COCOMO (Constructive COst Model) performed by Center for Software Engineering. First published in 1981, the original COCOMO model has recently been superseded by COCOMOII, which reflects a number of improvements.

*http://www.sikt.hk-r.se/~iqgroup94/view/cqm0908.html*

General outline on what a development plan should contain. (Web site is discontinued, but still points to the existing content.)

*http://huxley.baz.com/kjordan/swse625/htm/spmp_0_1.htm*

Software project management (SPM) plan for the MJY team (from George Mason University) that can be used as a resource for information. This web site also supports Software Risk Management.

*http://www.cs.msstate.edu/*

The software project management plan by the Department of Computer Science of the Mississippi State University.

*http://user.cs.tu-berlin.de/%7Efetcke/metrics-sites.html*

The *Software Metrics Sites* are a guide to Internet resources on software measurement, process improvement and related areas. Topics featured include electronic papers, bibliographies and conferences on software measurement, object-oriented metrics, Function Point Analysis and software process improvement.

The *Software Metrics Sites* list research institutes and people who are active in the area of software measurement. Several mailing lists that are used for discussions and the exchange of ideas can be found as well. You can locate software measurement tools that are available for download. The site also lists some sites that offer commercial products, and consulting and training services.

# 6 Experience Reports

O. Bécart (ed.)
Editions HIGHWARE

## 6.1 Selected Projects

Among the PIEs examined by EUREX and involved in the workshops, several particularly significant PIEs were selected for a more in-depth analysis (see Table 6.1). Their experience is both interesting and relevant to many of the key issues involved in software project management.

Table 6.1 The selected PIEs

| Project nr. | Acronym | Title |
|---|---|---|
| 21397 | EQISOMM | Formal Methodology for Software Application Maintenance |
| 23795 | PROMASYS | Project Management System for Formalising Software Development Projects |
| 21162 | ENG-MEAS | GQM Based Metrics for Risk Reduction |
| 21712 | VERDEST | Experimenting Changes the Development Process |
| 21415 | AMETIST | Formal Process Development |
| 23699 | DECO | Improved Project Estimation |
| 24287 | MASLYD | Software Cost / Estimation Processes and Life Cycle Definition |

The ESSI Dissemination Action SISSI (see 2.4.1) has looked at these projects as well. The introductory statement given by SISSI is cited in the following paragraphs.

In the domain of the information technology as in other business domains, a key success factor is product quality. Quality means the set of characteristics and the performance of the product. Of course, the quality of a delivered product depends heavily on the quality of the software development process. The quality of software development depends on the manner in which the various development activities are conducted:

• These activities have to be defined and scheduled before starting;
• Checkpoints have to be set.

To improve quality, four projects considered by SISSI proposed interesting search directions:

- Project Management System for Formalising Software Development Projects
- GQM Based Metrics for Risk Reduction
- Experimenting Changes the Development Process
- Formal Process Development

The success of a project depends largely on good project planning. Good planning comes from the definition of the project and how to do it (that is, the definition of the lifecycle). Two projects considered by SISSI deal with these questions:

- Improved Project Estimation
- Software Cost / Estimation Processes and Life Cycle Definition.

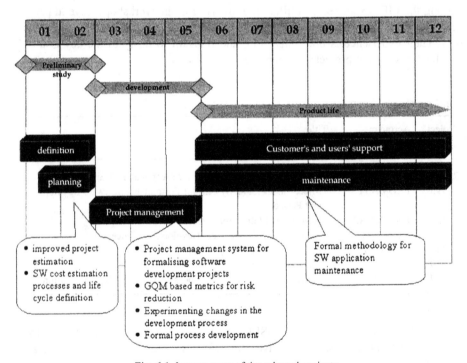

Fig. 6.1 Impact areas of the selected projects

In the following sections, we present relevant portions of the final project reports of the projects listed above.

## 6.2   Formal Methodology for Software Application Maintenance

### 6.2.1   Scope

The successful implementation of a maintenance methodology at PROFit (main contractor) and BFE (associated partner) has led to build up a people independent maintenance process and obtain the real maintenance costs, thus allowing the right resource allocation, and reducing in about 25% the maintenance costs. In particular, PROFit has managed to shift skilled and experienced people from maintenance to marketing support activities.

### 6.2.2   The Business Management System Market

PROFit Gestión Informática S.A. is a Spanish software house with more than 300 people and a 10 years experience in these three business areas:

- Development of software projects
- Consulting

   Moreover PROfit is the Gartner Group representative for Spain and Portugal

   PROFit develops and markets software products in the financial, retail and business management sectors, and adapts them to customer requirements. The fact that the maintenance is not carried out systematically causes frequent problems in the control of the different software versions.

   In the Banco de Fomento Exterior (BFE) there are two financial applications developed in house with own resources and the support of external consulting companies which, in certain cases have imposed some of their methodologies and tools.

   The documentation of applications is often quite different from reality.

   In both companies, PROFit and BFE, the maintenance activity is resource and cost intensive, and in the case of PROFit it uses highly qualified people,. required for other important functions (e.g. sales support).

### 6.2.3   Optimising the Maintenance to Improve Business

Based on above-mentioned maintenance constraints, PROFit carried out this process improvement experiment – the installation of a formal maintenance method – aimed to:

- free up the staff with more technical and business experience from maintenance.

- provide a people independent maintenance process (not requiring high qualified staff, and of a low training cost)
- introduce a methodology, techniques and quality criteria in an area usually poorly systematised.
- obtain the real maintenance costs and hence decide the most cost effective way forward.
- enhance process and data structures so as to rectify maintenance "black holes".

Another motivation for developing a people independent maintenance methodology, was to be able to carry out maintenance outsourcing projects.

The results were very positive:

- A net reduction of monthly maintenance costs of about 25%.
- A one year payback for the investment (in training and documentation).

### 6.2.4   Work Performed

The EQISOMM experiment consisted in developing and implementing a Maintenance Methodology (processes, circuits, phases and procedures) aiming at carrying out the maintenance activity by people independent of the development process, allowing the mix of different types of persons. The project started in January 1996 and lasted 12 months.

#### 6.2.4.1   Baseline Project

The experiment was carried out on two different baseline projects:

#### The Software Product Project
It was a software package called AUTODEX, a system for producing a dictionary of applications with various Y2000 improvements.

The team for this baseline project consisted of:
- 2 functional analysts with more than 5 years of experience in development and maintenance.
- 1 technology director for leading the project

#### The in house Application Project (BFE)
It consisted of two BFE own developments for financial applications (LOANS and CURRENCIES departments). The documentation was almost non-existent, hence their maintenance was completely people dependent. Both systems were in production at BFE.

### 6.2.4.2    Phases of the Experiment

**First Phase**

In order to have a better understanding of the maintenance problem a "Current situation analysis" was carried out. The activities consisted in the compilation of documentation about the applications. The documentation contained basically:

- Principal business functions
- Logical data and process models
- Physical models
- Current maintenance workload
- Estimation of the current costs

**Second Phase**

The circuits and procedures required for the control and processing of requests were implemented, and personnel freed up. It was also planned to take measures of the maintenance tasks, to obtain data of the personnel costs and to estimate the cost savings gained after restructuring.

The main steps in the development of the new methodology were:

- Identification of activities and intervinents (repeat and improve) and definition of the maintenance business process.
- Methodology for the standardisation of the maintenance process, based on Quality and Software Engineering criteria.
- Trial period, to follow-up the activities aiming at assuring the results of the project and introducing the function points estimation technique, software maintenance outsourcing and service level agreement

Two main yardsticks were established:

- End of the implementation process, to verify the process status.
- End of the trial period, to compare the obtained results against the expected ones.

## 6.2.5    Results and Analysis

Before  analysing the project results it has to be pointed out that there were some problems in the staff re-allocation process, due mainly to the lack of experience in considering various aspects of the "resistance to change", despite the fact of the stated re-allocation guarantee.

### 6.2.5.1   *Business and Organisation – Return on Investment*

The in house applications project is the one for which it is considered that a comparison process is relevant because the initial and final situations are similar in terms of baseline project.

The cost of the maintenance activities in BFE for the Loans and Currencies areas was 60 M$ (Portuguese currency).

Four high level people full cost 40 M$ approximately. Substituting these people for analyst-programmers with 2-3 years of experience provides 18 M$ in annual costs savings.

The proportional part of the new maintenance co-ordinator (currently 8 M$) has to be added to the costs, plus the documentation, restructuring and training costs (a practitioner analyst/programmer with two/three years of experience needs 2 to 3 months training period to be ready for the maintenance activities under the new methodology).

So, it is considered that the reductions in costs were absorbed during the first year by above stated additional costs. The benefits, therefore, start from the second year:

- costs reduction by change in staff level
- productivity increase by application of the new methodology
- process improvement, higher margins, and increase in competitiveness, without affecting to the company stability

In the case of BFE, a correct resource assignment to the different business activities has been achieved, thanks to the decomposition of the maintenance costs in corrective, evolutionary and preventive maintenance.

For both projects (Software product and In-house Financial applications) the results were very positives:

- A net reduction of monthly maintenance costs of about 25 %
- A one year payback for the investment (in training and documentation)

It is also important to say that at the end of the of the project the totality of high level staff had been replaced.

### 6.2.5.2   *Technical*

The implementation of a formal methodology for maintenance was achieved, based on a efficient documentation system, covering from the business process to the organic modules, allowing the replacement of the high cost staff within the planned time period.

Furthermore, the systematic recording of system activities made possible the planning and management of the whole process, determining costs and finding out the areas in which the maintenance was excessive.

With respect to the software product AUTODEX all highly qualified people has been shifted to sales support activities. The package is now compliant with year 2000 requirements, thus improving PROFit's marketing position.

The tables below show the relationship between the expected and obtained results in PROFit (Software product) and BFE (Financial applications). (Note: Upper number represents the objective, lower number the obtained result).

| OBJECTIVES | MONTHS | | | | | | | | | | | | |
|---|---|---|---|---|---|---|---|---|---|---|---|---|---|
| | 0 | 1 | 2 | 3 | 4 | 5 | 6 | 7 | 8 | 9 | 10 | 11 | 12 |
| 1. (N° Maintenance staff) | 4 | | | | 3/2 | | 2/1 | 1/1 | | | | | 1/0 |
| 2. (Months for training) | 3 | | | | 2,5/2 | | | 2,2/2 | | | | | 1,5/1 |
| 3. (% method implanted) | 0 | | | 20/30 | | | | 60/80 | | | 90/90 | | 100/90 |
| 4. (% main. cost reduction) | 0 | | | 0/0 | | 20/10 | | | | | 20/20 | | 25/25 |
| 5. (N° posibilities - % cost reduc. by re-engineering) | 0 | | | | 2-30/2-0 | | | | | | | | 3-50/6-0 |

**Fig. 6.2** Expected-obtained results/ Package solution project (PROFit)

In the case of PROFit nearly all objectives were reached, sometimes going beyond the expectations, with the exception of the fifth one. After analysing the results it was realised that two main circumstances led to this situation: one was the fact that the person in charge of the product, AUTODEX, left the company and the second one was the big workload in maintenance of the system at that moment.

In the case of BFE, as it can be seen, the objectives were broadly reached, with the exception of the increase in productivity by re-engineering which was smaller than expected. however, the productivity has increased overall and it is now easier to substitute maintenance personnel

### 6.2.6    Lessons Learned

The following key lessons have been learned:

• It is very important to present short term results in order to help keeping the management support which in fact is essential for the success of the project.

| OBJECTIVES | MONTHS | | | | | | | | | | | | |
|---|---|---|---|---|---|---|---|---|---|---|---|---|---|
| | 0 | 1 | 2 | 3 | 4 | 5 | 6 | 7 | 8 | 9 | 10 | 11 | 12 |
| 1. (N° Maintenance staff) | 4 | | | | 4/5 | | 3/4 | 1/2 | | | | | 0/1 |
| 2. (Months for training) | 3 | | | | 1,5/1 | | | 1,5/1 | | | | | 1/1 |
| 3. (% method implanted) | 0 | | | | 20/20 | | | 60/70 | | | 90/90 | | 100/95 |
| 4. (% main. cost reduction) | 0 | | | | 0/0 | 20/10 | | | | | 20/30 | | 25/25 |
| 5. (N° posibilities - % cost reduc. by re-engineering) | 0 | | | | 2-30/2-10 | | | | | | | | 3-50/2-30 |

**Fig. 6.3** Expected-obtained results/ Financial applications (BFE)

- Attention must be paid to take into account the human resistance to change.
- It is not possible to implement a discipline from the bottom.
- The implication of the managers is fundamental.
- The implementation of a new methodology is not well supported until the persons which have to use it can see and feel the real progress.
- The changes in people responsibilities must be carefully planned and directed by the managers in order to assure the success.
- Good experience is required to implement a metrics program in a short period of time.
- The maintenance must be considered as another activity of the software life-cycle.
- The implementation of metrics is a medium and long term road, and is dependent on the environment.
- To be competitive it is necessary to break down and classify the different maintenance tasks with the purpose of knowing which are the important parts and which can be reduced.

## 6.2.7   Future Actions

- The reinforcement of the maintenance business line is a competitive advantage derived from the EQISOMM project. In this sense PROFit expects to increase this activity from the present 10% up to 30%, with the inclusion of software maintenance Outsourcing activity, establishing contracts which include SLA (Service Level Agreement), Quality metrics, etc.
- It is expected to obtain actual savings from the reengineering options supported by the methodology, based on the continuous recording of information from the different activities.

- With respect to the maintenance of financial applications it has been decided to extend the method to more applications, since the standardisation and the costs reduction are strategic actions for the BFE.
- it is planned for next year to extend the new methodology to the whole maintenance department of PROFit.
- As a general future action it is planned to increase the commercial activity towards the European Union, actively promoting the attainment of projects for the European Commission in the areas of: Software Best Practices, Leveraging actions, etc., bearing in mind that the objective of PROFit is to devote to R&D activities the equivalent to a 3-5% of the total turnover.

### 6.2.8    Comments

Rafael Curiel Fernández, PROFit : "The application of formal methods in the software maintenance can represent up to 25% savings in maintenance related costs. In the future the productivity increase will be based in the reduction of maintenance costs."

PROFit Gestion Informatica S.A. is a medium size Spanish software house employing over 300 people. It is based in Madrid, with delegations in Barcelona, Santander and Lisbon (two tele-working centres operate in Bilbao and Valencia). The turnover for 1997 was 18 MECU, with an estimated of 24 MECU for 1998.

## 6.3    Formalising Software Development Projects

### 6.3.1    Scope

The implementation of a Project Management System (Methods and Tools) has permitted to steer and manage the development of the logistics and production management system Project, deploying additional resources as required, avoiding delays and meeting user expectations on time and quality. In our experiment the weighed average of the difference between planned and actual effort was 8%.

### 6.3.2    Software Development in a Production Plant Environment

Gonvarri Industrial S.A. is an important Spanish group in the steel transformation industry. The EDP structure is based on an AS/400-RPG/400 and Windows-NT/Visual Basic shop.

Primary activities of the software development department deal with the updating and maintenance of the logistics and Production management system.

However, new requirements arise constantly, forcing the company to develop high quality software very quickly.

Main software problems were the following:

- The applications were people dependant
- Lack of formal software engineering methodology.
- Software development not supported by CASE tools.
- Difficulty in project tracking.

Further to that, a major set of improvements to the logistics and production management system were planned.

### 6.3.3    Business Objectives and Motivation

The above-mentioned situation pushed Gonvarri to the implementation of a Project Management System, while developing the improvements to the logistics and production management.

The Promasys experiment was aimed at defining a well-structured Software project plan system, establishing a clear set of commitments between software developers and users, and clarifying the tracking of Software Projects.

- The main objectives of the experiment were to:
- Achieve a 15% maximum deviation in size estimation of projects and development sub-products.
- Achieve a 15% maximum deviation in effort planning and scheduling.
- Achieve a 5% maximum deviation (days) in delivery time of software products
- Establish beforehand the resources and skills required.
- Establish attainable commitments with internal and external clients.
- Provide the management with the means for periodic project reviews and tracking.
- Ability to measure the success of Software Development Projects in terms of cost, timeliness, performance and quality.

The most significant results achieved are reported in table 6.2 below.

### 6.3.4    Work Performed

The phases of the experiment were the following:

#### Workpackage 1: Implementation of the Basic Infrastructure.
The main activities carried out during this phase were:

**Table 6.2** Significant results

| Objective | Achieved | Target | Comments |
|---|---|---|---|
| Deviation in effort estimation | 8% | 15% | 8.8% is the weighted average. Deviations of more than 15% were recorded (see section "Results and Analysis") |
| Deviation in delivery date estimation | -5% | 5% | Products were delivered 5% earlier than planned |
| Project tracking procedure | ☑ | | |
| Project reporting and control process | ☑ | | |
| Establish beforehand the resources and skills required | ☑ | | |
| Establish commitments with the clients | ☑ | | |

- Definition of common ground between senior management and user representatives in order to achieve an agreement on the objectives and scope of the project, thus gaining their support.
- The Promasys Team undertook training on project management concepts and tools.
- Deployment of supporting tools.
- A deliverable was produced, containing the software project control organisational aspects, and the communication and reporting procedure within the organisation.

### Workpackage 2: Definition of a Well- Structured Project Plan.

As a result of this phase the document "Project Plan structure" was produced, containing:

- The guidelines to settle the objectives and scope of the project. A "Project proposal" was prepared based on these guidelines, describing basically the:
  - Objectives and scope of the project
  - Main business functions affected
  - Business impact.
- A guide for planning software projects. It contains the procedure to define the components of the initial conceptual design, which must be one of the results of the basic engineering phase.
- The procedure to define the contents of the products and the criteria to break-down the work.
- Definition of the metrics for effort estimation. Initial effort was dedicated to understand and customise the "function points" metrics, but finally it was de-

cided to base the estimation methodology on a predefined set of "reusable components", which is well known internally.

### Workpackage 3: Establishment of the Commitments.

A final version of the commitment method was achieved by including some changes suggested by the users. The agreement was represented as a standard Project Plan (an MS-Project Document) with the following main characteristics:

- The different phases of each project are always the same and are perfectly clear for both parties.
- Phases are subdivided into tasks with enough level of detail as to be meaningful for the developers and at the same time understandable to the users.
- The control tasks, as well as the Milestones are included in the plan.
- Each task has assigned:
  - Estimated hours of effort.
  - Assigned resources.
  - Start and finish date.

### Workpackage 4: Establishment of Project Tracking.

The tracking structure was finalised, and somehow reshaped all the other elements of the Project Management Method. For example, tracking or control tasks are now included in the Standard Project Plan. The reporting procedure has been updated and the role of the Organisational Structure reformed in order to make it more agile and capable of steering the project. Major highlights are:

- In the Standard Project Plan, the Milestones and the Roles of the participants in the decisions are clarified.
- Validation of the Catalogue of Requirements by the users involved.
- The Basic Engineering Phase to be approved by the Planning and Steering Committee.
- The final System should be validated against the Catalogue of Requirements. This validation should be done in the presence of the users.
- The planning committee should formally accept the delivery of the system before putting it into production.
- The project manager reviews the progress of the project on a weekly basis. If the deviation of the project against the plan is greater than 10% (for the current phase), it should be notified to the Planning and Control Committee.

An assessment of the tracking of the Baseline Project has been produced.

### Workpackage 5: Preparation for Further Improvements.

As a result of the work performed during the development of the Promasys experiment, various major improvement initiatives are being carried out, or are under study. These initiatives are described in the last section of this document "Future Actions".

## 6.3.5 Results and Analysis

At the beginning of the experiment, three very clear objectives were established for the Project Management System, as follows:

- The number of days of deviation between the scheduled and actual dates of product delivery should not be greater than 5% of the total product development time.
- The difference (in person-days) between the planned and actual effort required to deliver a product should not exceed 15%.
- The difference between the estimated and actual product size, once developed, should not exceed 15% (measured in function points).

The results of the experiment according to the first two objectives are summarised in the following tables:

**Table 6.3** Analysis of deviations- Effort

| Phase | Initial Estimated Hours | Actual Spent Hours | % Deviation |
|---|---|---|---|
| Project Definition | 40 | 48 | 20% |
| Basic Engineering | 148 | 143 | -3,3% |
| Detailed Engineering | 221 | 236 | 6,7% |
| Construction | 411 | 450 | 9,5% |
| Pilot test and kick-off | 60 | 74 | 23% |
| Follow-up | 120 | 137 | 14,1% |

As we can see in tables 6.3 and 6.4, the accuracy of the estimation has been variable along the development life cycle, both in terms of effort devoted to the project and precision in the delivery dates.

Various key lessons can be extracted when analysing the tables:

- If we take a look at the table at a global level, the results are:
  - The weighed average of the differences between the planned and actual effort was 8%, therefore meeting the objective of less than 15%.
  - The weighed average of the differences between the planned and actual delivery dates was 5%, which is also a value within the objective of a 5% maximum deviation.
- The real conclusion, however, can be extracted only by looking at the details. If we take a closer look at the results, we can see that all the estimations related to the users were simply wrong. For example:
  - The definition of the project took 20% more than planned.
  - Integrated testing took 39% more than planned.
  - Approval of the pilot project took 28.5% more than planned, etc.

**Table 6.4** Analysis of the deviations- Delivery time

| Phase | Initial Estimated Working days | Actual Working days | % Deviation |
|---|---|---|---|
| Project Definition | 6 | 8 | 33.3% |
| Basic Engineering | 22 | 20 | - 10% |
| Detailed Engineering | 23 | 25 | 8.5% |
| Construction | 62 | 55 | 11.2% |
| Pilot test and kick-off | 10 | 10 | -9% |
| Follow-up | 13 | 15 | 15.3% |

On the other hand, the estimations of the technical work were rather accurate (building confidence in the estimation method based on Reusable Components).

In any case, all these figures point to what, in Gonvari's management opinion, has been the key result of the experiment:

"By using the Project Management System we were able to steer and manage the development of the "Electrocincado" project, deploying additional resources when it was required, avoiding delays and meeting the expectations of the users on time and with a high level of quality".

There was a third objective regarding the product size estimation, measured in function points.

This method has been discarded in favour of another one based on reusable components developed in house. This is basically a way to formalise and capture knowledge that the developers already have.

Although the first results are promising, further accumulated experience is nevertheless needed in order to guarantee its accuracy.

Other results achieved have been:

- Capability to establish beforehand the resources and skills requirements.
- Capability to establish attainable commitments with internal and external clients.
- Providing the management with a way to periodically review and track the progress of software projects.

### 6.3.6   Lessons Learned

The following key lessons have been learned:
- The clarification of the objectives and rationale for a project should be carefully done before launching the project.
- A controlled environment allows for real management of the projects.
- Internal knowledge should be re-used.
- Estimation metrics are very difficult to apply and might be misleading.

- Not to be obsessed with the accuracy of the metrics but to use them as a valuable reference guidance; it is a lot better to have a reference with a 20% of deviation than not having any.
- It is very critical to re-assess software development effort in light of the continuous change in the business environment, balancing the needs of the end-users with the real needs of the company as a whole.
- It is very important that all the parties involved agree on the schedule.
- By developing the projects within a controlled framework, it is easier to negotiate with the users the real priorities and their proper delivery dates.
- An appropriate organisational structure should be in place.

### 6.3.7 Future Actions

Post-Experiment actions have been launched as follows:
- A major revision of the IS planning process will be made in order to formalise it and align it to real business requirements.
- Implementation of a Configuration/Change Management System to follow-up the development and the usage of reusable components.
- Implementation of a Quality Program for the whole IS department based on "Service Level Agreement".
- The deployment of an Object Oriented Software Development environment is being seriously considered (as a direct consequence of the application of the "Reusable Components" method)
- The generalisation of the "Project Management System" is occurring. All new projects are launched within the framework settled by Promasys.
- A "simplified" version of the project management system is being developed to cover software maintenance. In fact, the project tracking application is already being used to control maintenance tasks. If we are able to follow-up the maintenance process adequately, it is foreseen that a large percentage of this function could be outsourced thus freeing experienced programmers to work in new projects with a higher value.

### 6.3.8 Comments

Carlos Piqueras, Organisation & Systems Manager : "A major improvement to our logistic and production management system comes from having software projects realistically planned, managed and under control."

Gonvarri Industrial, S.A. is a family owned, value added, steel producer with a vocation for permanence and long term development. The number of employees in 1997 was 1273, with 30 of them devoted to software development. The strategy of the company relies on offering new services to the clients, with a high level of quality (Gonvarri has received important recognition, such as the Volkswagen "Value to the Customer" Award and the Ford Q-1, among others).

## 6.4    GQM Based Metrics for Risk Reduction

### 6.4.1    Scope

The successful introduction of a measurement program at Engineering Ingegneria S.p.A. using the Goal-Question-Metric paradigm and completed by refined statistical analysis techniques has allowed to identify the main factors affecting effort and productivity. As a consequence, better project estimation and tracking have contributed to project cost reduction (8% estim.), risk reduction (20%) and increased customer confidence.

### 6.4.2    Project Control in Distributed Organisations

The world-wide crisis of the software market also affected the Italian market in which Engineering operates. Nonetheless, Engineering reacted very well to that crisis, as is proved by the continuing growth increase in revenues and employment.

However, Engineering suffered and still suffers a *dramatic reduction of profits*.

Furthermore, the ever-increasing risk associated with the *growing weight of large turn-key projects* with respect to the other lines of products represents another crucial point to be taken into account.

In this context one of the most important problems – if not the most – affecting project development and profitability is the *geographic distribution* (a strategic choice of Engineering) represented by 11 local units taking both commercial and technical responsibilities.

To overcome this situation, which is characterised by factors such as:

- lack of project control capability
- difficulty in human resource interchange
- need for better relationships between central functions and production teams

actions had to be taken to unify and standardise the Software Production process.

### 6.4.3    Process and Product Metrics for Precise Project Control

Motivated by the need to provide managers with effective support in predicting and controlling the software process, Engineering selected the "Goal-Question-

Metric" method, as the most suitable and successful way to tie the measurement program to the organisational goals and objectives.

ENG-MEAS has made possible to accept contracts measured in delivered function points.

The following main choices were included in the experiment:

- introduction of Function Points analysis
- systematic definition of the measurement plan through the GQM method
- adequate statistical procedures for data analysis.

The results of the project can be summarised as follows:

- the commercial risk has been reduced by an estimated 20%, due to better project estimation and reduced guarantee cost
- it is possible today to assign people to work on projects in other regional units
- the project tracking tool has become a strong competitive advantage for Engineering.

### 6.4.4 Work Performed

The project lasted 18 months, between January 1996 and June 1997.

A working group, formed by people from the various departments, was in charge of:

- performing the initial assessment
- defining the GQM plan
- defining the measurement plan
- analysing data, and refining the GQM and measurement plans

#### 6.4.4.1 Assessment of the Current Scenario

In order to better focus the objectives for the subsequent phases, an initial assessment was conducted, giving the following main results:

- Explosion of the technological environments used in the company's projects. Consequences:
  - difficult for project managers to use past experiences
  - need to understand and control the spread of different technologies
- No systematic collection of data on the size of the developed software system
- Weaknesses in productivity evaluation:
  - No precise measure of the effort expend during the guarantee period was available
- No meaningful indicators for defect rates:
  - There were no standard and suitable measurements available to assess the quality of the development process and the effectiveness of each life-cycle

phase, such as: number of defects, nature of defects, originating phase, finding phase, cost to fix, etc.

### 6.4.4.2    Definition of the GQM Plan

The GQM plan, which is the most important product of the GQM paradigm, was produced within the framework of the following guidelines and constraints:

- the purpose of characterising the development process with respect to productivity and defectiveness
- the analysis was the only focus on the product line represented by turn-key projects
- the analysis was intended to focus on the technical aspects of the projects only
- the focus was on the phases specifically devoted to software development (Conceptual Design, Technical Design, Realisation, System Test & Delivery, Guarantee)
- the focus was on variation factors that might have a significant effect.

A GQM plan is defined in terms of:

- **Goals**: a goal is defined in terms of: an Object, a Purpose, a Quality focus, a Viewpoint, and an Environment)
- **Abstraction sheets**: composed of Quality Focus, Variation Factors, Base Level Hypotheses, and Impact on Base Level Hypotheses
- **Questions**: derived from the abstraction sheet in order to define and to characterise the goal in an operational way
- **Metrics**: derived from each question, and used to collect data in order to answer the questions

### 6.4.4.3    Definition of the Measurement Plan

For each metric identified in the previous phase, it was determined when, how and by whom the metric data have to be collected and who validates and stores the metric data.

Two adequate baseline projects were selected, allowing to monitor two critical aspects detected in the initial assessment: guarantee period, as a "black hole" and the absence of meaningful measure of defect rates.

### 6.4.4.4    Refining the Plans and Analysis of Data

An independent review of the GQM plan produced revised versions of the measurement programme.

In order to identify those projects which deviate significantly from other projects, either by being extremely good or extremely bad, a Bivariate Anomaly Detection Analysis was used.

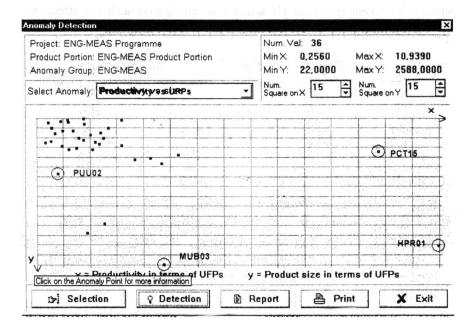

**Fig. 6.4** Graphical results of the Anomaly Detection
X axis: Productivity in terms of UFPs,
Y axis: Product size in terms of UFPs Anomaly detection results

## 6.4.5   Results and Analysis

### 6.4.5.1   Technical

#### GQM Results

The basic GQM plan defined two goals, with the following Quality Focus:

- GOAL 1: Productivity at the delivery end and at the end of guarantee
- GOAL 2: Process defectiveness/Data analysis

Analysis of project productivity, through a specialised data analysis procedure based on stepwise analysis of residuals, has identified that the *main statistically significant factor affecting productivity* is development environment generation (third, forth and RAD). This factor accounts for 47% of the variation.

The model based on the above variable plus: *effort, size* (measured as Unadjusted Function Points) and Unit site, accounts for 83% of the variation.

To provide some check on the productivity model (to prevent the   possibility of spurious relationships due to the fact that size and effort are functionally related to productivity) a similar analysis was performed, using effort as the dependent variable. This analysis revealed that only size (55% of the variation) and development environment generation (10% of the variation) have statistical effects on effort.

### Bivariate Anomaly Detection Analysis

Bivariate anomaly detection has been used to identify those projects which deviate significantly from other projects.

(In Figure 6.4 for instance, PUU02 project is identified as a project of relatively Low Productivity for its size. It was due to the fact that the project went through a very formal and documented development process.)

### 6.4.5.2    Business

Although a complete assessment of the impact on the business will be possible only with the prosecution of the measurement program, it is already clear that:

- a 20% reduction achieved on the commercial risk of the projects
- development costs have been reduced by approx. 7/8% due to the faster reaction to field error correction, and a significant improvement in effort/time estimations
- the overhead for project teams is less than 2% and is seen as acceptable by the management
- net margin has been improved by approximately 10%
- the effort for central measurement staff is limited to 2-3 person-years
- impact on commercial aspects
  - after the ENG-MEAS project, the company is in the position to tackle those tenders in which payments are related to the number of delivered Function Points
  - the measurement programme, when it becomes visible to the customers, helps to make transparent the supplier-client relationship and to qualify the supplier.( As an example, a customer choose to participate in the defect analysis improvement task).

### 6.4.6    Lessons Learned

### 6.4.6.1    Technology Point of View

The main key lessons learned from this experiment can be summarised as follows:
- the introduction of the measurement programme must follow a gradual approach: do not try to measure everything at the initial stage of the project
- the top-down systematic approach enforced by GQM is very effective in achieving a consistent measurement program
- project team members must be convinced of the reasons for measurement: they must be informed in advance
- knowledge on Statistical Analysis is required to better analyse specific measured data

- Function Points: its adoption as a software sizing metric has been suggested by technical and commercial considerations

### 6.4.6.2   Business/Organisation

One of the weak points that emerged concerned the errors produced in the application of the contracts, due to the Project Manager's  lack of knowledge in the administrative aspects.

To overcome this a campaign has been launched in 1997 to shift the training efforts from the Technical estimation  towards  Contract management.

This "97 Contract Management campaign" is expected to definitely be helpful to manage the large turn-key projects in which sub-contracting represents approx. 50% of the total amount.

To tie the measurement program to the company's organisational goals and objectives is the key to make "useful" the program itself.

Specific attention must be devoted to derive "simple and comprehensible" measures. This will help to overcome such problems as communication between Technical and Commercial staff.

### 6.4.7   Future Actions

The company is committed to continuing and enlarging the measurement program. The main development lines foreseen are:

- to characterise new software development phases for improvement
- to improve the analysis of the origin of the errors
- to offer Consulting services on Measurement and Statistical techniques  to our customers, aiming to gain competitive advantage.

*The Quality System is no more seen as a document management system but an effective measured-based control and improvement system*

### 6.4.8   Comments

Nicola Morfuni, Engineering Ingegneria Informatica commented: "By monitoring values and trends of major variation factors for our software development process, we obtained a better risk management on large turn-key projects and a more effective staff/skill allocation."

Engineering Ingegneria Informatica SpA is a large private Italian software house with more than 560 employees and a turnover of 60 MECU in 1996. Engineering is the Head of the Engineering Group, which has 1200 people and 90 MECU turnover (1996).

## 6.5  Experimenting Changes the Development Process

### 6.5.1  Scope

After experimenting with object-oriented technology the Regional Government Services group with TT Tieto Oy have implemented a working system to ensure take-up of new technologies through the rest of the group.

### 6.5.2  Having to Adopt New Technologies

In order to meet customer demands for improved functionality, or even new products, many companies need to incorporate technologies from third parties. This can be done for a variety of reasons:

- need to respond quickly
- shortage of internal resources
- need to reduce development costs.

As a result of having chosen specific external technologies, many companies find that the knowledge of using them becomes tied up with the key individuals who performed the developments. Only a few will have climbed the often steep learning curves of the new techniques. By having this knowledge concentrated in one place, there are several questions the organisation should ask:

- what happens when the key individuals leave?
- what happens when other staff try to climb the same learning curve?

### 6.5.3  Responding to Customer Needs

In this case study TT Tieto Oy needed to address the demands of their customers for systems that had different price/performance ratios. They did this by incorporating a third party package into their software that allowed seamless access to different database systems.

The knowledge they gained from this exercise allowed the group to re-use the code to produce a new version of the software in 40% of the time of the original software development.

The group have also recognised the need to share knowledge through the company in order to help develop new products and make changes to older legacy systems. As a result they have introduced a software technology centre of excellence to perform this task.

### 6.5.4   Why Perform the Experiment?

Due to perceived customer demand, the regional government services group within TT Tieto Oy wanted to be able to provide a variety of different pricing solutions for its customers of the PALLAS software for libraries. They intended to do this by using different priced database systems in which information was stored by their application.

However for maintenance and productivity reasons the group did not want to produce multiple ports to different databases. Therefore the group decided to adopt a third party software component that would allow the underlying database to be changed according to customer requirements whilst leaving the core of the system relatively unchanged.

However in order to do so it would require that the group move towards a C++/OMT based methodology in order to incorporate the component software that was accessible only through C++.

Within the baseline project of the Process Improvement Experiment the group applied the new techniques to an Open Public Access Catalogue (OPAC). This would give them a project that was sufficiently demanding but was not mission critical to the business.

### 6.5.5   Project Results

#### 6.5.5.1   Ability to Use Different Databases

The project succeeded in replacing the underlying database through the use of component software and the group were able to demonstrate the use of Ingres, Oracle, MS Access and dBase databases without the need to change any source code. This allowed the group to offer differently priced applications with different levels of performance – so broadening their potential customer base.

#### 6.5.5.2   Fast Reaction to Customer Demands through Re-Use

After seeing the release version of the OPAC software the customers came back with additional features that they wished to see. This necessitated writing a version of the software to be client/server based.

By re-using the existing code but replacing the database access routines to become client/server based the group were able to produce a system with 40% of the effort of the original software development.

- Incorporation of 3rd party component software: 221 days
- Re-write to incorporate client/server model: 91 days.

### 6.5.6    Lessons Learned

#### 6.5.6.1    Experts are Important

During the project the company worked with an external contractor who acted as an "expert". After the project this link disappeared and the group had to continue gaining experience by itself. According to Kari Malinen, Software Director, *"The biggest lesson we learned was that the company needed experts to make the new techniques work, we therefore changed our business process to incorporate a centre of excellence and allow for the "right" people to be able to share their experience in applying the new technologies with others and give expert advice."*

As a result of the setting up of the centre of excellence, new product development is originated within the group with the aim of rolling out their expertise into the rest of the company. An example of this is a new World Wide Web (WWW) based version of the OPAC that was developed using the experience of the group on the client/server system produced in the project.

#### 6.5.6.2    Adopting New Methodologies are Not Easy

Tieto were aware of the "philosophical" step between third generation (C) and object oriented (C++) languages. However due to the steep learning curve of C++ Kari Malinen felt that "there was often a conflict between becoming proficient in the new language with the new technologies and meeting the demands for fast results to demonstrate to the clients". According to Juha Pakkanen, Project Manager, *"following the demonstration of the prototypes to the clients, large changes were often needed and we found it difficult to do this quickly enough with C++. It was easy for the developers involved to lapse back to the old C based procedural methods that "worked" in order to achieve a solution."*

### 6.5.7    The Importance of Selecting the Right Tools

During the project the group used Visual C++ and component software called odb++. Due to initial bugs in these systems the group spent a significant amount of time overcoming the problems. Because the group were working in a new language and programming methodology they often found the task even harder.

However since completing the project, the group have moved to development using Java and Delphi. Juha Pakkanen feels that *"these new tools hide a lot of the problems we had had with C++, as a result of fewer implementation problems the theory of object orientation clicked into place for many of the current team members."*

### 6.5.8 Comments

Kari Malinen, Software Director: "By experimenting with new software techniques we have been able to re-think our development process and recognise the need for experts in technology areas. This has lead to at least one new product for the group."

The Regional Government Services group within TT Tieto Oy are a software group supplying a variety of different application to local government, schools and libraries. The group employs 170, of which approximately half are software developers.

## 6.6 Formal Process Development

### 6.6.1 Scope

By adopting defined software development processes and by introducing quality assurance and documentation procedures, R.O.S.E Informatik GmbH were able to reduce delivered errors by 60%. They saw an improvement in SYNQUEST assessments of 200% as a result of the PIE.

### 6.6.2 Productivity Preserved

For small companies that enjoy good flexibility and high productivity, it is easy to view the implementation of formal procedural and documentation measures as a low priority. In fact, the introduction of such measures may be heavily resisted on the grounds that they may harm the creativity of a team and make it less efficient. It may be thought that a free-form approach will be more rapid because staff can concentrate on the project in hand as opposed to following guidelines and completing administration.

It can be seen, however, that the introduction of structures such as software developmental procedures can be of enormous benefit to small companies. These benefits can be seen in a variety of ways, some of which are unexpected. For example, the introduction of measures, which at first sight are time consuming, can end up saving a company time and improving profitability. The measures need to be incorporated in a sensitive manner: the cost of implementation is high for a small company and there needs to be careful management of expenditure.

The experience gained here will be of use to any small software company attempting to make the transition to become a professional software house.

### 6.6.3   Creativity and Control

As a small company wishing to develop and grow, R.O.S.E. had several target areas upon which it wished to improve; these had been highlighted by the SYN-QUEST assessment. They included the fact that R.O.S.E. did not have a defined process of software development and that there were few records of work performed. These issues become increasingly important as a company grows in size since fault tracking and procedural issues become more complex.

At the beginning and the end of the experiment SYNQUEST assessments were performed and they showed an improvement of about 200% towards a process oriented company.

R.O.S.E. Informatik develop Knowledge Based Software Products for the functional analysis of complex systems. The disciplines represented include Computer Science, Physics, Mechanical Engineering and Medicine.

Another desire of the company was to obtain ISO 9001 certification: the PIE would be an important step in this accreditation.

The company had attempted implementation of a common development method before, but this had been unsuccessful. In addition there was great resistance to change within the company; people believed that the most appropriate way of dealing with large and complex problems would be the same as  the way in which the company had dealt with smaller, simpler ones. For these reasons, the PIE was very useful: it enabled a smooth introduction to a new methodology.

### 6.6.4   Work Performed

There were four main tasks, which the PIE aimed to achieve. These were:

- The introduction of a quality assurance system.
- The implementation of  a good software development process.
- A documentation system.
- A method of measuring and evaluating quality.

The process started by defining what was needed in each of these areas and preparing the software development procedure. Each of these measures was then implemented on an average software project for the company. Finally, the improvements achieved, and changes noticed, were analysed and the information was disseminated.

R.O.S.E. is a company with a small number of employees: all members of the company were involved with the PIE. Everyone had been involved on the project and helped to work on the experiment even it was difficult to obtain consensus on the exact form of the new development process.

During the PIE, the company introduced a Lotus Notes system, which dealt with the new documentation procedure. Further databases were set up in Lotus Notes to deal with the quality assurance and measurement requirements. This set-up means that project proposals can be followed all the way through to their execution using a single system. It can also be used to monitor errors on a project and requests for changes by customers.

Due to the fact that the company is so small, training was not a major organisational problem. Development of new processes involved all people who were involved in it. Communication took a variety of forms including email, scheduled meetings and spontaneous discussions.

For each aspect of the project, a person from the team was assigned as an expert. This person received the basic training and then made useful information available to other members of the team. The staff mainly learned the new techniques and methods by a hands-on approach. Information was also disseminated using the new documentation system.

### 6.6.5 Project Results

The main benefit of this project was the reduction in the number of errors in software delivered to customers by 60%. In addition to this, self-assessment results covering issues such as the number and effectiveness of processes in place were improved by 200% at the end of the PIE than they were at the beginning.

Engineers in the company have seen that less time is spent on maintenance of software systems. Additionally, the information required for the work is organised better, both for individual employees and for the team as a whole. This means that tasks no longer are forgotten and that the information required for a project is available to the relevant engineer rapidly.

The result of the PIE on communication within the company has been marked. Previously virtually all communication between team members was verbal, whereas now much of it is done using the new administration method.

Before the PIE, many of the members of the team had no skills regarding the software development process, but during the course of the experiment many of the staff learned important techniques necessary in order to understand and manage the development process for a piece of software.

The initial scepticism about changing the method of operation was a difficult barrier to overcome. The PIE was very useful in this respect and helped convince many members of the team that as the programs that they develop become larger and more complicated, so their internal processes must become more sophisticated.

The effect of these changes to the business has been that the company can now supply its customers' requirements more precisely because their initial project definition process is better documented. In addition to this, since time monitoring is part of the documentation system, it is easier for them to calculate the billing for a project.

### 6.6.6   Lessons Learned

R.O.S.E. found that many of its engineers had perceived the best route to high productivity to be working hard on their own. In fact, this style of working results in lower overall productivity. This is due to the fact that the productivity of other engineers suffers to such an extent that it affects the whole team.

The company discovered that although time may be lost during the actual implementation of new procedures, it is more than made up for later on when the benefits of the process begin to appear. They also found that new methods have to be introduced simultaneously with new tools-it is no use a team having advanced technology if they use it in an inefficient manner.

From a more business-oriented perspective, they found that their company has been strengthened. Due to the benefits of the PIE, their projects are now better thought out, more efficient and of higher quality. They found that the difficulties encountered in changing the ethos in the company was at least partly due to the fact that the existing measures had been in place for a long time. In R.O.S.E.'s experience, a new software company should introduce a development methodology as early as possible in its life in order to avoid encountering these problems.

R.O.S.E. found that its small size was a mixed blessing in carrying out the project, it made the distribution of the information more straightforward, since official dissemination had been unnecessary.

### 6.6.7   Next Steps

Consolidation and further development of the methods and processes introduced in this project are expected in the future. In addition to this, it is hoped that the PIE will be an important step towards the gaining of ISO 9001 certification, which should enable the company to attract more custom.

## 6.7   Improved Project Estimation

### 6.7.1   Scope

Engineering Ingegneria Informatica S.p.A. succeeded in improving the accuracy of their project estimation (manpower, cost and elapsed time) through improving their software engineering. This was achieved by building a database compiling their experience gained in earlier projects. The result was to reduce the average estimation error from 25% to 8%.

## 6.7.2 A Key Business Lever

Project estimates are a key business lever, and are vital for any company when budgeting, planning and managing investments in software applications. There is great motivation for business managers to improve their project estimation, as any improvement which can be made has a direct impact on the business.

Project estimating is important for companies producing software (both for in-house use and for sale by software companies). Bad estimates can lead to missed delivery dates, over-budget use of resources and inefficient project management.

Accuracy in estimations is particularly crucial for software companies to rival increased competition. When tendering for business an estimate which is too high loses the business, whilst one which is too low makes the business unprofitable.

Businesses which buy in tailor made software should ask their software suppliers about the rigour of their project estimation.

## 6.7.3 An Improvement Approach

In this case study the Italian company Engineering faced the problem and achieved an improvement in their estimates of 60%. Average deviations were initially 25% and went down to 8% (ranging from -10% to +10%) in six projects in which it was applied.

**Table 6.5** Project estimation error

| Results | Initially | Achieved |
|---|---|---|
| Average project estimation error | 25% | 8% |

The approach was to extend their development methodology to cover the formal specification of non-functional requirements (such as ease of use, reliability and portability) so that the impact of these could be traced throughout the development process. This then sets up a self-reinforcing cycle, where better knowledge of these impacts leads to ever-better estimation and project planning.

The cost/benefit threshold is 250 000 ECU projects. Any company developing (either for internal use or for commercial purposes) software applications of that size or greater can benefit from this experience.

### 6.7.4   Project Estimation Errors

One of the main reasons behind Engineering's decision to carry out this project was the fact that too many projects were running over their initial estimates made during the commercial negotiations resulting in lost opportunities for profit.

Engineering develop in a wide variety of environments (dependent upon the client's target environment) for a range of differing applications. As such, it has access to extensive data about how the development activities vary not only dependent upon the environment but also in relation to the client's non-functional requirements such as ease of use, reliability and so on. However, this data was not being structured in a systematic and useful manner, meaning that a potential source of competitive advantage was not being exploited.

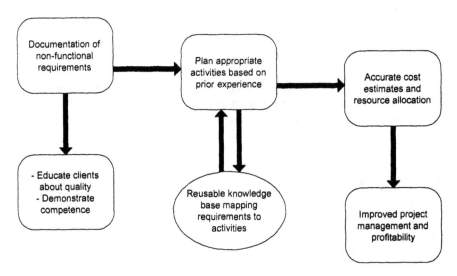

**Fig. 6.5** Engineering's Strategy for Project Estimation Improvement

### 6.7.5   Before Improvement

Before the improvement project was carried out, the average error in project estimation was approximately 25%, a figure calculated from a sample of ten representative projects. Typically, projects took more time than had been anticipated, and in one case a huge error of under estimation by 76% had occurred, which had a huge effect on Engineering's project management and resource planning activities.

### 6.7.6 Results

The project was very successful, with the accuracy of the estimation process improving very significantly. From an average estimation error of 25% (varying between - 76% and + 12%) over 10 projects prior to the experiment, the average error decreased to just 8% with a variation between - 11% and + 12% in six projects following the introduction of the methodology extensions.

*"Before this project, our average error varied from -76% to +12%."*

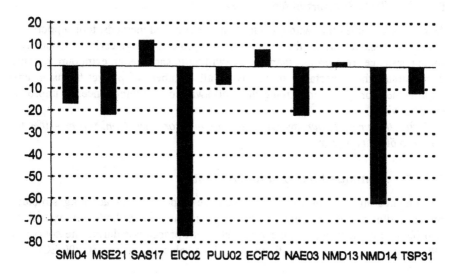

**Fig. 6.6 % Error in estimation – Before Experiment**

This project has had a very real effect on Engineering's business and their relationship with their customers. The methodology which Engineering applied has been presented to key customers and has met with a very positive response.

### 6.7.7 Lessons Learned

Engineering learned a number of important lessons in the course of this project.

#### 6.7.7.1 The Methodology cannot Always be Applied

One of the lessons which Engineering learned is that in real commercial situations, it is not always practicable to obtain the information necessary to make a detailed activity plan. Sometimes there is simply not enough time to do so before a proposal deadline.

### 6.7.7.2    A Minimum Worthwhile Project Size

Any structured approach implies an extra effort over ad hoc approaches. Engineering found that the improved estimation accuracy and other benefits of the methodology extensions were not worthwhile for projects with a value of less than 250,000 ECU.

### 6.7.7.3    Tool Support is Necessary

As many companies find with the adoption of structured methods, tool support is a critical success factor. In the course of this project, Engineering encountered some resistance from project managers unwilling to shoulder an extra burden. This demonstrates the importance of involving all members of project teams in any improvement process, and making them all aware of the importance. of improvement activities.

*"After the project, our average estimation error varied only from -10% to +10%, a 60% improvement."*

### 6.7.7.4    Continued Use of Improvements

For Engineering, this project has proved the importance of adopting structure project estimation and planning methodologies. The new methodology extensions will be incorporated into Engineering's standard procedures during the course of 1996. They will be applied to all projects with a value exceeding 250,000 ECU.

### 6.7.8    Future Plans

Engineering are continuing to improve their process planning techniques. Work has begun on improving automated support for a knowledge-base to address the issue of the extra overhead that it imposes on project planning. In addition, Engineering is now undertaking a major new metrics project to examine the project lifecycle in more detail and determine the most suitable objective measures for progress. In this way, they continue to benefit from their investment in software best practice.

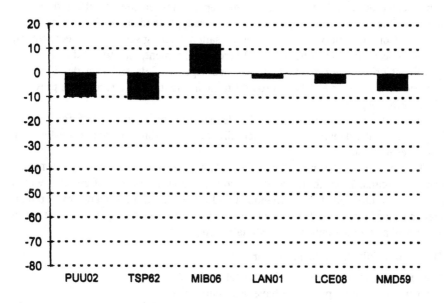

Fig. 6.7  % Error in Estimation – After Experiment

## 6.8    Software Cost Estimation Processes and Lifecycle Definition

### 6.8.1    Scope

I.C.E. Computer Services Ltd were heavily dependent on key staff within their software division. In addition, cost estimation was an area of concern to the company. As a result, of a planned quality system, which was based on a defined life cycle, I.C.E. were able to tackle these problematic areas. The company is benefiting, having noticed a 57% increase in software installation sites.

There are a large number of small multi-disciplined organisations that offer a range of business services including software development. Although these type of organisations have strong software divisions, their software/IT competence often lies with key staff who develop software through their own undefined procedures and practices. Companies operating in this type of structure often find it difficult to disseminate knowledge internally, and if those key individuals leave, it can have a devastating effect. Also there is a third dimension to the problem, namely, it is difficult to implement a software process  in a company that has no defined procedures and practices in place, and particularly so where randomly evolved practices are present. In these organisations there is often the need to implement processes that can reduce the dependency on the specific individuals and allow the company to operate in an organised, planned and efficient manner.

I.C.E. Computer Services Ltd, an organisation offering services for recruitment, computer/secretarial training and software development, identified the need for significant process improvement in various aspects of its software department's activities. This matter had been brought to their attention as a result of a previous "TRI-SPIN" project.

Firstly, the findings identified  the dependency on specific staff for product knowledge in the department, and secondly  the unreliability of the cost estimation processes in place.

The company recognised that it had major potential for growth in the next 5 years and realised that to achieve this growth, the current areas of concern would have to be addressed. I.C.E. developed and documented a software development lifecycle appropriate to their business needs. Based on the new lifecycle, they developed a complementary cost estimation formula.

The major results from the project are:

- an increase in software installed at sites by 57%.
- costing/estimating processes have been improved.
- dependency on key staff eliminated – this has been tackled by documenting the life cycle and software.

### 6.8.2   Work Performed

I.C.E. currently have two major  commercial software products in the market. The main product is a software package for Credit Unions, and covers all front-office and back office functions. The second major product is called SRMS Professional. This is aimed at the Staff Recruitment agencies and lets companies manage candidate records.

Using the data collected on I.C.E. time allocation and a pre-defined life cycle model, I.C.E. developed and documented a software life cycle appropriate to their environment, clients and products, supported by appropriate computer based project management tools.

The data collected during a defined period allowed them to identify their modus operandi. They then matched this data with the defined life cycle and identified the changes they needed to implement. An appropriate life cycle was then documented and implemented, and its success was reviewed and refined.

Since I.C.E.'s staff required education in the area of "Software Lifecycle", a training program was set up. This was delivered by an external consultancy, and consisted of general training on the various styles of software lifecycles followed by discussions on the relevance of each style to I.C.E.'s business.

Training in cost estimation algorithms was given to staff. This was delivered by an external specialist consultancy.

Current timesheets/project data were analysed to establish a baseline project. Based on the new life cycle the data collected was used to develop a cost estimation formula. The newly developed cost estimation algorithm was applied to the base line project for a limited time for analysis purposes. Any deviations were then noted and fed back. End results were documented to conclude what had been learned.

### 6.8.3    Project Results

The project has generated the following major results for I.C.E.:

- 57% increase in software installation sites
- Costing/estimating processes improved.
- No longer dependant on key staff – This has been tackled by documenting the life cycle and software.

Prior to the project, I.C.E. felt that they were unable to grow their software business. As a result of implementing the project life cycle in the department, they have been able to increase the level of business significantly. This is reflected in the fact that at the start of the experiment their main software was installed at 35 sites, but this figure is now approaching 55 sites and is still growing.

From a technical point of view, the development and application of the ICE-SCRAP function has been a tremendous success. The ICE-SCRAP function generates reports during enhancements to a system. As a result, I.C.E. can now quickly and    confidently assess the total impact of proposed changes to its software.

The area of bespoke development was a concern also due to the fact that there was no consistent approach to cost estimation. Now that  the cost estimation process has been put in place, bespoke development are  more in line in terms of contributing to the overall company profit.

This project has been of tremendous benefit to all personnel within the software development department. There was a definite trend of individuals showing interest as they became involved in relevant projects and experienced the benefits.

### 6.8.4    Lessons Learned

With this work, I.C.E. have learned that, by implementing and defining a life cycle process, they have been able to significantly improve aspects of the software development process. Furthermore, I.C.E feel software life cycle processes go hand in hand with other software related activities, for example, maximum development efficiency.

Originally, I.C.E. may have underestimated the amount of work required to perform the project. This is due in part to the fact that as they became more involved in the analysis process, they came across areas of concern that they had not originally anticipated. However, the experience has been positive, and now that they are seeing the benefits, they feel the project has been worthwhile.

The project leaders have changed during the project for unavoidable reasons, and although this has not created a major hurdle for I.C.E, they recommend assigning a team which can see a project through.

# 7 Lessons from the EUREX Workshops

O. Bécart
Editions HIGHWARE

This chapter consolidates results presented and achieved during the three EUREX workshops that focussed on project management. Two of these workshops were held in France, including the initial prototype workshop, and one was held in Britain.

Obviously, Process Improvement Experiments took place in various disparate environments and we tried to provide an atmosphere in which experiences could be shared.

We have made an attempt to model the workshop results into a unified prospective. This is presented at the conclusion of this chapter.

## 7.1 First French Workshop

### 7.1.1 Date and Place

Workshop 1 took place in Paris on January 29th, 1998, and acted as a prototype.

### 7.1.2 Scope of the Workshop: Learning from the Experiments

Scope of the workshop was focussed on generic learning to be made from experiments:

- Has the business got profit from process improvement?
- Is the solution defined for process improvement appropriate for the business?
- What are the causes leading to process improvement?
- Which business drivers and priorities did lead to undertake a process improvement experiment?
- Where are failure factors of process improvement?

Then, PIEs were presented by speakers.

## 7.1.3  Minutes

It first started with a presentation of the EUREX scope and purpose. Some discussions occurred on the ESSI program itself and first expectations of non PIEs participants were to see which learnings may come out.

### 7.1.3.1  PIE : Intelligent Simulation Environment Development

ESSI Project 24149 – PROMISED – contractor: CSTB-M Werner Keilholz

- Business sector: Construction and Building
- Application Area: Simulation Environments
- Key Word: ISO-SPICE assessment
- Project objective: the PROMISED experiment aimed at increasing the maturity level of CSTB development process from its current status to a higher level of maturity.
- Expected Impact: improvement of CSTB development process. Impact of tested solutions needs to be measured in relation to their costs. This information will help define the factors involved in respect of a quality approach for business software development activities.

#### Presentation of CSTB

CSTB is a 600 people company, including 300 engineers and research workers. It has an annual budget of 340 million French Francs, split as follows:

- 35% research and development using public funds
- 25% scientific and technical consultancy
- 30% evaluation and certification
- 10% dissemination of knowledge

The Software Evaluation and Valorisation Division, in charge of PROMISED project, is made of 15 people and is part of the IT and Construction Department, which counts 50. The IT and Construction Department is located in Sophia Antipolis (in the area of Nice, South East of France).

#### Aim of PROMISED

The aim of PROMISED is to improve development processes using the future ISO SPICE standard.

ISO-SPICE, which is not really a certification model, has been designed to evaluate Software Processes. This model provides not only an evaluation but also a method of ongoing improvement of the various processes concerned. The fields of applications of this tool are: Acquisition, Supply, Development, Use, Maintenance, Support.

**PROMISED Context**

Projects are of various size (1 to 3 developers and 10,000 to 150,000 lines of code). The environment is heterogeneous (PC and UNIX workstations).

Table 7.1  PROMISED Approach

| Action | Result |
|---|---|
| 1 – Carry out initial evaluation | initial process model |
| 2 – Draw up plan of measures to be taken | measurements plan |
| 3 – Apply measures and analyse | new process model |
| 4 – Define new target (level of maturity) | evaluation results |

The experimentation was carried out internally for some projects. The experimentation tool chosen is CONCERTO, a tool produced by SEMA Group (France).

**PROMISED Results Achieved so far**

Evaluation of CONCERTO: the tool is too cumbersome, and is not adapted to a non-homogenous environment. The EVL Division now uses traditional tools (word processor, email, MS Project, Access, etc.).

Evaluation of SPICE: the tools show adapted to the context (small team, trainees, subcontracting).

The results given by the individual presentation of the PROMISED PIE leads to the following: below which threshold, and which size (number of projects under way, duration, number of people), does SPICE remain applicable?

- 1.5 years < duration < 3 years
- 5 < number of people < 20 to 30

The result of this experimentation (CONCERTO and SPICE) has been disseminated to the Division other projects and to other CSTB teams.

### 7.1.3.2    PIE : Conception of Object-Oriented Reservoir Simulator

ESSI Project 24182 – COORS – contractor: IFP/ Daniel Rahon

- Business sector: Research and development in Petroleum Industry
- Application Area: simulation of physical phenomena (fluid flow in porous media)
- Key Words: Object Oriented Development, Simulation Software, re-use, POSC
- Technologies / Methodologies / Tools: Object Oriented technologies, OMT, CASE tool IFP counts 1,850 employees, 185 are involved in software production, 10 of them focus on fluid flow simulators.
- Project objectives: IFP is a research institute that produces software which is then industrialised and commercialised by specialised companies. The experi-

ment is the complete realisation of an object oriented library of business classes for the petroleum industry and its integration in a numerical fluid flow simulator.

- Expected impact: One of the aims is to reduce the costs of software development by producing reusable components and the costs of industrialisation by writing programs close to their industrial version.

Another objective is to experiment the use of object oriented technologies at IFP to ensure required flexibility in IFP programs to continually integrate new results of ongoing research and to manage the complexity of the physical models represented.

### COORS Context

IFP (Institut Français du Pétrole) is a research institute serving oil and automotive industries.

IFP researchers produce algorithm-type software. IFG subsidiaries then market these.

Between these two phases, IFP observed substantial differences between industrial version and research version. Product upgrades are costly: how to perform software evolution at lower cost?

The basic project consists of designing a simulator of fluid flows in oil fields: this development project uses complex physical and numerical models (>500,000 lines of code).

The experiment consists in introducing new technologies linked to object oriented development through a small program named SIMTEST.

SIMTEST is a digital simulator of single-phase fluid flows: this development project uses simplified physical and numerical models.

### Aims

- Assessment of impact of object oriented technologies used by researchers.
- Assessment of object performances under simulation.

### Involved Parties

These are researchers specialising in fluid flow simulation, a specialist in object oriented programming, and an expert consultant specialising in object modelling.

### Why to Use Object Oriented Technology ?

Object oriented technology has following advantages:

- better mastering of complexity when developing large software programs
- in-built capacity to evolve and be maintainable for cost-saving
- reusability: the trade classes library offers services that can be reused by researchers

- easier interchange between various software programs dedicated to a single trade

IFP internal culture and working methods arose following issue: changing tools has not been encouraged, and capitalisation at the trades level has been poor.

### Aims
- to avoid redeveloping existing tools,
- to have a common working structure,
- to have support structures: an objects library for each metier.

Together with the objective of decreasing production costs, by offering well-designed, and therefore saleable, software.

### Technical Aspects
The POSC (Petrotechnical Open Software Corporation) is a consortium which develops methodologies and tools (data models) for software development projects.

Epicentre is an example of a data model.

Purpose is to promote reuse by designing trade objects modelled using Epicentre, and then, to install POSC software for each class of trade.

### Conclusions
Reuse must be integrated right from start of the project. There are several levels of reuse of components and modelling, which imply that visibility will be a requisite: hence drafting of very exhaustive documentation.

It is difficult to draw up a document giving complete specifications that will enable another team to perform design.

In addition, moving on to design is a more difficult phase for researchers.

Researchers are asked to play several roles at the same time: acquirer, developer and user in their research function. There is an overlap, as the researcher seeks, creates and uses. Different cultures are involved, and the researcher is not the best model of co-operation.

The culture of the user is completely different from that of the software developer.

Problem for researchers is to trace original brainchild in the final program.

The other issue is the written word culture. There is a significant need in terms of data modelling.

POSC is more structuring than mere transition to the object, but problems arise when all the objects are connected together.

The following question came up: when does number of object data start to make connection difficult? By common consent, it is agreed that the limit of simplicity is the number that can be counted at a glance: roughly 7 objects give or take another two objects: more than that, complexity is considered.

Summary: Achieve models to combine complexity.

### 7.1.3.3   PIE : Geographical Information Systems On O2

ESSI Project 10515 – GISMO – contractor: 3IG – Mme Françoise Liard

- Business sector: IT Integrators, End User
- Application Area: Information and Geographical Software Environment
- Key Words: Object Oriented Analysis and Design, Object Data Base Management Systems
- Technologies / Methodologies / Tools: Object Oriented technologies, ODBMS 3IG sells URIAH, a GIS development environment. Main customers are located in French Government Agencies, defence sector and industry.
- The objective of the GISMO project is the evaluation of Object Data Base Management Systems (ODBMS) used together with an Object Oriented Analysis and Design (OOAD) approach in the area of Geographical Information Systems applications.

GISMO intends to improve Object Oriented technology: to design a CASE TOOL enabling complex objects handling.

The experiment has been carried out on small internal applications.

GISMO project is the opportunity for 3IG's group of developers to learn how to use object oriented design and development technology which is expected to increase the efficiency of the software engineers and the quality and flexibility of the development.

### Results

After the CASE TOOL development:

- some basic concepts were missing to establish all models,
- the CASE TOOL has too few applications to be used internally,
- documentation time saving: more comments in programs, which enabled to speed up documentation process,
- problems arising during development phase were recognised more quickly,
- focussed more on development quality than on definition quality.

### 7.1.4   Conclusions of Presentations

After individual presentations, the following questions came up:

- Why has practice improvement been engaged?
- Which are practice improvement failure factors?

Each of these questions has been discussed, and the outcomes show hereafter.

## Question 1: Why has Practice Improvement been Engaged?

Answers which came up were:

- the market (competition)
- the environment, the offer (technological change)
- smaller budgets
- reduced time frames
- lack of internal skills

Then, each rapporteur had the opportunity to identify which process improvement driver promoted the project (showing in hatched on the diagram):

**Table 7.2**  Process improvement drivers

| Drivers / PIE | PROMISED | COORS | GISMO |
|---|---|---|---|
| market | | | |
| offer | | | |
| budget | | | |
| availability | | | |
| internal skills | | | |

## Question 2: Which are Practice Improvement Failure Factors?

Outcomes of the subsequent exchanges are summarised here:

- fear of change
- rigidity of the organisational structure
- immature technology
- ignorance of available techniques
- absence of strategy
- absence of a decision-maker
- necessity for change not recognised
- lack of means
- unavailability of human resources

Just like for question 1, each participant had then the opportunity to locate one's own environment in this list of risk factors.

For table 7.3, conventions are:

- Hatched grey box: the factor is troublesome for the business,
- Plain grey box: the factor is not present, quite the opposite.

Table 7.3 Process improvement failure factors

| Failure factors / PIEs | PROMISED | COORS | GISMO |
|---|---|---|---|
| Fear of change | | | |
| Rigidity of the structure | | | |
| Immature technology | | | |
| Ignorance of available techniques | | | |
| Absence of strategy | | | |
| Absence of a "champion" | | | |
| Necessity for change not recognised | | | |
| Lack of means | | | |
| Unavailability of human resources | | | |

## 7.2  Second French Workshop

### 7.2.1  Date and Place

Workshop 2 took place in Aix-en Provence (France) on June 3rd, 1998, and focussed on validating the model that had been designed during workshop 1.

### 7.2.2  Minutes

Unfortunately, an air traffic strike prevented a number of participants to attend the workshop. A majority of them had to cancel their participation the day before. A limited number of attendees focussed on the results of a survey that was lead between the two workshop with French and Belgian PIEs.

Written contributions to the workshop had however been received that enabled to draw the following conclusions:

#### 7.2.2.1  PIE : 21814 OOSA

ESSI project 21814-OOSA, contractor: SA INTELLECT-PRODATA NV

At the time of the contribution, the project was still in progress, and no public communication had been engaged yet. Then its results were not formalised enough to enable firm conclusions.

However, following process improvement drivers have been identified:
- Market evolutions,
- Budget decrease,
- Timeframe decrease,
- Lack of internal skills.

For all these four process improvement drivers, project management and estimation have been recognised to be major improvement directions.

Addressed process improvement risk factors have been the following:

- Fear of change,
- Immature technology,
- Unknown technology,
- Poor perception of needed change.

These risk factors have been addressed through the PIE as follow:

- Fear of change: bringing evidence that change is not harmful by an actual project (would it be a dummy project).
- Immature technology: increase level of skill through training, but results that have been achieved remain limited.
- Unknown technology: keep a continuous information (reviewing press and underlining key articles and news).
- Poor perception of needed change: increasing communication between technology departments; this particular issue may have been addressed in a better way, if available metrication results had been distributed.

### 7.2.2.2 PIE : Process Improvement Experiment of a Code Generator

ESSI project 21710 – PICGAL (Process Improvement Experiment of a Code Generator), contractor: AEROSPATIALE

Contribution from PICGAL stressed that formal methods and related impacts on lifecycle had been pulled by the following business drivers:
- Market evolutions,
- Suppliers offer evolutions.

Addressed process improvement risk factors have been the following:

- Immature technology,
- Unknown technology,
- Lack of means,
- Human resources not available.

Reportedly, the PIE, as run and funded in the frame of the ESSI program, had been an adequate answer to these risk factors.

### 7.2.3 Discussion and Conclusions

During the workshop, discussion first addressed the issue of software projects overrunning timeframe and budget.

Feedback by expert was that most of the problems were to be traced back to the original fuzziness of the project launch: a clear view and common (and shared) understanding of scope of the project was a key project success factor. Then, methods to model operations, automations and software design were of great help.

Another opinion was shared by a consultant who is a recognised specialist in software project value analysis was that when defining a project problems that are encountered appear to be technical issues while human factors and communication issues are actually the main source of inconsistencies. Technical modelling may be used as language to prevent actual human problems to come to light. Then, value analysis showed to be efficient to map the various problems.

Then, results from PIEs were reviewed (both from workshop 1 and PIEs contributions from those who could not attend the workshop).

Conclusions were to reword process improvement drivers and process improvement risk factors consistently as presented in the workshops summary.

Then a new issue has been discussed concerning the number of risk factors in a process improvement action.

It may seem pure common sense, but observed reality shows that the lowest number of risk factors would prevent dispersal in improving a software process, and thus ensure success. The point is that process improvement mainly deals with human aspects: addressing a few (if not a single) improvements is more easily acceptable and feasible than a number of.

Consequently, process improvement is perceived more efficiently if addressing as few process improvement drivers as possible. The one shot process improvement is too academic, it is supposed to fix all business drivers at the same time, to incorporate a single new technology and to get involvement of software developers. Such a goal would come together with too many risk factors that it would never be met.

A step-by-step process improvement, showing actual intermediate results is key. Thus there is a need for strategic planning of process improvement.

How to perform a process improvement strategic plan is an issue that is of highest interest for managers, consultants and researchers. And there is a strong demand for that.

Now, will ESSI program provide enough materials to construct such process improvement strategic planning technology? Could be. At least, it would provide a number of tips, how to's, and not to do's. This was both a wish and an expectation.

Ideally, business drivers analysis should lead to wording and prioritisation of process improvement strategies. Communication on these should ensure commitment and undertaking of the various role players. Then technologies should be selected and training together with experiments planned. Process improvement should then be managed in such a way that risk factors should be addressed properly. Each step to be then assessed: achieved results and goals met. Then, a new step to be lead and the overall strategic process improvement plan assessed against its compliance to business situation.

## 7.3 First British Workshop

### 7.3.1 Date and Place

Workshop 3 took place in Claverdon, Warwickshire on April 14th, 1999, and was intended to conclude the series of workshop run on Estimation, Project management and Lifecycle.

### 7.3.2 Minutes

Like in previous workshop, context and objectives were introduced, then PIEs were presented.

#### 7.3.2.1 SIMMER1: An Improved Method for Cost Estimation and Project Tracking

Brian Chatters
ICL, United Kingdom

The following starting scenario was first presented:

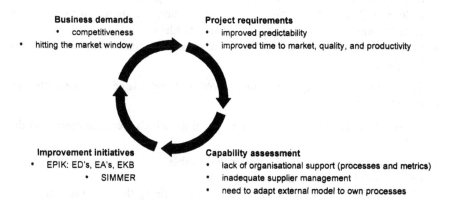

**Fig. 7.1** Starting scenario

Then the theory CMCP (Cellular Manufacturing Process Model) was introduced:

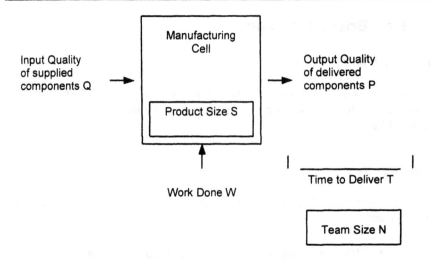

**Fig. 7.2** CMCP Cellular Manufacturing Process Model

Metrics related to the CMPM were presented:

- Input Quality Q: The proportion of the requirements on the input components that are met without cost being incurred in the integration cell.
- Delivered Quality P: The proportion of the customer requirements on the integrated product that are met by the delivered product.
- Size S: The size of the delivered and consumed components in "Standard Integration Units"

The SIMMER Experiment was then introduced and related measurements were commented.

These results were generalised into key learnings which were presented and discussed:

- Each cell needs a formally controlled deliverable.
- Projects need to run for at least four months.
- The method provides a structured approach to defining the work products
- Manage the causes rather than the effect.
- Provides a catalyst for process improvements to improve the quality of the incoming components.
- It is vital that the experience database is populated with historical data.
- If a problem is encountered with a supplied component, significant delays can occur in the project's schedule.

Eventually, the following conclusions were shared:

- The CMPM provides a more effective means of planning and tracking software and systems integration projects that are dependent upon components supplied by third parties.
- Involvement of staff from the baseline project has ensured that the method is acceptable and can build on existing practices.
- The method is sufficiently flexible to be deployed across any organisation. It is particularly applicable to small to medium size projects.

### 7.3.2.2 PIE : Improvement of Effort, Cost Estimation and Cost Control

ESSI Project – 23962 COCOSPIE – contractor: Philotech GmbH.

Making a reliable tool-supported effort and cost estimation method an inherent element of our software development process is important for our company, especially as Philotech is mainly a software vendor, developing customer software systems in the area of Aerospace and Medicine technology and Defence. To achieve this goal, Philotech was conducting its process improvement experiment COCOSPIE which consisted of the following steps and actions:

- selection of an cost estimation model and tool (COCOMO II , USC COCOMO)
- training of the staff on software project management, effort and cost estimation, cost control, and metrication
- data collection (analysis of previously completed projects to be used for)
- tool calibration
- validation of the calibrated tool on the Baseline Project
- establishing a Project Database.

### Weaknesses of the Project
Data collection turned out to be difficult as data and metrics of completed projects have for several reasons not been available to the expected extent. Therefore the process of Tool Calibration was based only on a small number of projects with the result that the estimation tool was only coarsely calibrated.

### Strength of the Project:
The training performed during the project has provided the staff with a profound knowledge about software effort and cost estimation which helps executives to identify cost drivers during the development process and to make more efficient use of the available resources.

For the data collection phase a data collection questionnaire and a metrics measurement plan have been established. Both will be used in the future for data and metrics collection on all software development projects. With these collected data the Project Database which was build up during the ESSI project will be maintained, resulting in an increasing and broader amount of data which will improve the cost and effort estimation.

### Conclusion

Though the ESSI Project suffered from several weaknesses the overall results of the experiment were positive and the activities started will be continued to make the effort and cost estimation an inherent element of our development process.

### 7.3.3    Summary and Conclusions

Then, workshop continued with discussion on process improvement risk factors. Results consisted in both identification and marking (considering 10 is highly critical, when 0 means low impact):

- Lack of commitment: 10
- Lack of monitoring/feedback: 10
- Unable to quantify business benefits: 9
- Shifting environment: 7
- Prefer to invest in technology and tools rather than methods: 4
- Don't know where we are going: 3
- Resistance to change (or "fear of the unknown"): 3
- Don't dare to remove processes (e.g. in Space and Safety-Critical System): 3
- Short-term versus long-term trade-off's: 2
- Don't understand or like the word "process": 2
- Changing minds later (Some changes have a short lifetime): 1

Then, remedies were assessed. Table 7.4 summarizes this discussion.

**Table 7.4** Risk factors and identified remedies

| Risk factor | Identified remedies |
|---|---|
| Lack of commitment | • everyone is to win, <br>• get real involvement (NOT a directive). |
| Lack of monitoring/feedback | • no proposed actions to improve this problem. |
| Unable to quantify business benefits | • need rapid positive experiences, <br>• need real related experiences (perhaps via internet communities). |
| Shifting environment | • need visionaries. |
| Prefer to invest in technology and tools rather than methods | • no proposed actions to improve this problem. |
| Don't know where we are going | • visionary to provide an alternative. |
| Resistance to change (or "fear of the unknown") | • need to experience it, <br>• provide education. |

| Risk factor | Identified remedies |
| --- | --- |
| Don't dare to remove processes (e.g. in Space and Safety-Critical System) | • no proposed actions to improve this problem. |
| Short-term versus long-term trade-off's | • pick the cherries from the cake,<br>• need visionary and intrapreneurs. |
| Don't understand or like the word "process" | • avoid using the word? |
| Changing minds later (Some changes have a short lifetime) | • no proposed actions to improve this problem. |

## 7.4 Conclusions Drawn from Workshops

### 7.4.1 Process Improvement Drivers

Improvement means a change: an original status and a target one. In process improvement, both original and target status are processes. The way people are performing certain tasks is being changed. A process is changed because the original process doesn't adequately match the organisation's priorities. It is considered implicitly that the process matched the organisation at one time. Then, something changed the organisation's priorities and the process is no longer satisfactory. Whatever made this change appear is what is named here a change driver.

More precisely, the change has been designed to increase consistency between the process and the new organisation or company priorities. Better consistency is covered by improvement.

Process improvement is expected to increase consistency between how people perform certain tasks and the priorities of the organisation they work for.

The reason why is then named Process Improvement Driver (PID).

Considering the field of project management, estimation and lifecycle, the applicable process areas cover what people do in order to make software projects shorter and/or less resource consuming.

Many companies and organisations engage in many activities intended to reduce the timeframes and budgets of their software projects. The main process improvement drivers have been found to be:

- PID 1: competition in the market that urges them to be at least as reactive (if not pro-active) as their competitors,
- PID 2: the environment of the offer (new technologies) that enable their suppliers to provide more and more integrated solutions; it is influenced by the growing complexity/diversity of software which requires integration with more and more partners, or become diverse multinationals,
- PID 3: a top management strategic trend to outsource development and maintenance of software that is not a key part of the core business.

Other process improvement drivers may also exist, such as making software more reliable, or increasing users comfort and satisfaction, but with regard to the fields of project management, estimation and lifecycle, the EUREX workshops focused on these three above.

A common problem in making software projects shorter and/or less resource consuming is answering the question "shorter than what?" or "less resource consuming than what?" Smaller than expected or smaller than committed? A client or a user may either expect a software project to be completed within committed timeframe and budget (in which case delays are the issue) or one may consider the committed timeframe and budget (which is named the baseline) are too large with respect to operational needs.

Making software projects shorter and/or less resource consuming as an issue is twofold:

- how to detect and correct delays, and
- how to set a realistic baseline.

Delay detection and correction is addressed by project management on one hand, and by lifecycle on the other hand:

- Lifecycle improvement to enable visibility and reactivity (prevention of both ballistic and tunnel effects).
- Project management improvement to ensure proper detection (and impacts) of delays, and then adequate decisions so as to strengthen up the project.
- Realistic baseline setting is addressed both through estimation and lifecycle:
- Estimation improvement helps to quantify a baseline that is consistent with the know how of the project team,
- Lifecycle improvement to set the project flow, which is optimum with operations constraints and needs.

The entire process improvement cycle is:

- Recognise new strategic requirement: process improvement drivers.
- For (all or part of) the requirements identified, investigate estimation, project management and/or lifecycle opportunities of process improvement (current process, potential improvements, available technologies and means).
- Run one experiment (Process Improvement Experiment – PIE), and then assess results.
- Deploy, and assess results against the original strategic requirement.

## 7.4.2  Process Improvement Failure Factors

At the end of the day, it may happen that the original strategic requirement is not met. In other words, the process improvement failed as a whole, either because it was a wrong direction in the first place, or the direction was correct but the improvement itself failed. It is very easy for process improvement to fail because human factors are paramount.

When a process improvement has been defined (what to achieve), it is important to do a careful study of what could make it fail (the process improvement failure factors) and how to prevent such failures. The EUREX workshops have been an opportunity to confront various failure modes and to summarise these.

When planning for a process improvement in the field of estimation, project management and lifecycle, it may be useful to perform a full risk analysis.

When we consolidated many of the PIEs that were funded in the frame of the ESSI program, the principal process improvement failure factors were discovered to be these:

- Fear of change: people would consider a change as a potential loss (of the original process) that may damage their future.
- Technology and tools rather than methods: process is key but process improvement may seem abstract and virtual.
- Rigidity of the organisational structure: the process improvement has not been recognised as effort and resource consuming in itself.
- Immature technology: the process improvement which has been engaged is based on a technology that was expected to be mature but that turns out not to be, at which point much effort and focus is spent on the technology itself and process improvement becomes secondary.
- Ignorance of available technology: the process improvement that has been initiated is based on a technology that is not appropriate.
- Absence of strategy: the strategic process improvement driver is either not clear or not commonly recognised.
- Shifting environment: one or more strategic process improvement drivers may disappear or change.
- Unable to quantify business benefits: lack of quantification to justify the process improvement as well as to measure compliance of the process improvement experiment with strategic improvement drivers.
- Lack of commitment: at any level of the organisation, lack of individual undertaking to meet the strategic process improvement driver. When resources are scarce, day-to-day life (high priority projects, support activities, maintenance, etc.) tends to absorb them and to deflect from process improvement tasks.
- Lack of monitoring/feedback: the process improvement has not been defined as a project in itself and/or is not managed by a single person; it is expected to take place just by providing technology and training.

Process improvement failure factors seemed to be consistent in many different environments and enterprises; however, cultural differences showed up in the prioritisation. For example, the EUREX workshops encountered differences between French and British PIEs in the ranking of the most critical factors. In the UK, the most critical failure factors appeared to be the following:

- Lack of commitment;
- Lack of monitoring/feedback;
- Unable to quantify business benefits.

On the other hand, in France the following were considered most critical:

- Rigidity of the organisational structure;
- Lack of commitment;
- Unable to quantify business benefits.

### 7.4.3    Process Improvement Success Factors

To avoid process improvement failure, we conduct actions and/or make arrangements intended to decrease the associated risks. These are named process improvement success factors.

The ESSI Process Improvement Experiments provided a good opportunity to identify a number of remedies and strategies to address process improvement failure factors. The following table 7.5 is a summary of these strategies.

**Table 7.5** Process improvement success strategies

| Failure Factor | Success Strategies |
| --- | --- |
| Fear of change | Providing training and education. Running one experiment (the PIE) to be used as an objective proof. Getting actual results of similar process improvements in other companies or organisations. Explicit statement of management of stakes and needs for change. |
| Technology and tools rather than methods | Using sophisticated tools bears value to people, but sophistication also means complexity. In order to decrease it, the introduction of sophisticated tools is supported by a description of simple ways to use them; the description of simple ways is another way of saying methods. Then, process improvement is supported by new tools introduction. |
| Rigidity of the organisational structure | Process improvement to be designed as a step by step. Each step being identified, planned and managed as a project. |
| Immature technology | Differentiating technology qualification and process improvement. Getting technology qualified first. Getting the commitment of people involved in process improvement experiment to focus on process improvement, and to identify technology problems separately. |

| Failure Factor | Success Strategies |
| --- | --- |
| Ignorance of available technology | Keeping technology transfer opportunities open (attending workshops, conferences). |
| | Keeping in touch with consultants committed to ensure technology compliance. |
| Absence of strategy | Process improvement to be designed as a step by step. Each step being identified, planned and managed as a project. |
| | Explicit statement of management of stakes and needs for change. |
| Shifting environment | Keeping a process improvement steering committee which would meet once every quarter or so, in order to review progress, results, compliance and re-orientation options. |
| Unable to quantify business benefits | Getting rapid positive experiences. |
| | Getting real related experiences (possibly via Internet community, conferences or so). |
| Lack of commitment | Designing and communicating value for everyone rather than issuing directives. |
| | Providing training and education. |
| | Explicit statement of management of stakes and needs for change. |
| | Running one experiment (the PIE) to be used as an objective proof. |
| Lack of monitoring/feedback | Process improvement to be designed as a step by step. Each step being identified, planned and managed as a project. |
| | Keeping a process improvement steering committee which would meet once every quarter or so, in order to review progress, results, compliance and re-orientation options. |

## 7.4.4 Conclusion

No Process Improvement Experiment in the project management domain addressing teams from various countries at the same time has been reported. As a result, multi-cultural dimensions did not show up directly in the PIEs; however, multi-cultural differences eventually do show up, and this has certainly been a major experience of the EUREX project.

# 8 Significant Results

G. Vallet
Editions HIGHWARE, Paris

Software Process Improvement in the areas of Project Management, Lifecycle and/or Estimation is founded on management decisions. Its success or failure is strongly related to its management dimension. In this chapter, we make some observations based on experience both in and out of the EUREX context.

It is worthwhile to note that there was quite a difference between feedback received from EUREX workshops in France and similar workshops in the UK. In France, the management dimension is understood as *what my manager should do* to support Process Improvement, while in the UK it is understood as *what I as a manager should do* to make Process Improvement successful. In other words, culture does matter.

## 8.1 An Important Process Improvement: Organise the Project Mode

"Project management, estimation, life cycle", these concepts are intertwined with the concepts of the project and of the organisation to lead projects: the project mode. EUREX deals with the project mode in companies.

A project is all those actions that contribute to achieving a defined, known and measurable result: the product.

The project mode consists in defining and identifying projects as such, and directing part of the company activity in such way that these projects succeed.

The aim is not to convert companies to the project mode: all activities dealing with software are not projects. Rather, the aim is to facilitate a change in corporate culture, which starts in the project mode, in most cases as a result of purchasing project-scheduling software.

### 8.1.1 Domains of the Project Mode

In a project mode operation, the individuals involved in a project undertake activities specific to the project. These activities are combinations of processes that depend on techniques. The processes and techniques are classified in seven domains:

1. Product definition: the appreciation of the result of a project as regards its adequacy, by criteria of price (cost), risks and value.
2. Project planning: the organisation of the development activities, as well as tracking and leading the project.
3. Project scheduling: the determination of the project timetable and associated resource schedules, as well as ongoing tracking of project progress.
4. Project leading: project co-ordination, as well as the detection and solving of non-completion and/or project non-compliance factors.
5. Multi-project scheduling: synchronised consolidation of progress status and schedules of various projects, the integrated scheduling of these projects (to solve conflicts when using shared resources) and the formulation of requirements for use of resources in each project.
6. Multi-project monitoring: the arbitration of conflicts in the use of common resources by various projects, and the insurance of correct completion of a series of projects.
7. Project steering: the decision to continue, redirect or cancel a project, based on criteria of qualifying the opportunity addressed by the project, and of re-evaluating the appropriateness of the solution (which is the result of the project).

### 8.1.2    Three Viewpoints of the Domains

#### 8.1.2.1    *Viewpoint of Those Using EUREX Techniques*

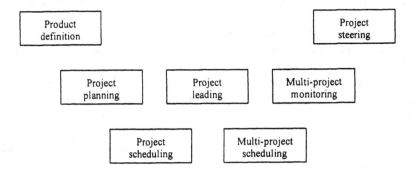

**Fig. 8.1** Project mode domains

Figure 8.1 symbolises the stages in the change in corporate culture towards the project mode.

The rationalisation of project mode operation is often initially regarded as a problem of project or multi-project scheduling. Management often says something like "to make projects work well, you just need to install some project scheduling software". Following this decision, the operational integration of project scheduling software is in itself an important step in the change of culture.

Then comes the question of the degree of confidence that should be afforded the results calculated by the project scheduling software (whether calculation assumptions correct and complete is a question of project planning), followed by the integration of these results in the project decision-making process (this is the domain of project leading and project monitoring).

Lastly, a key factor in project mode failure is the lack of consistency between the result of the project and the operational environment. This factor is addressed by product definition and project steering, and is very often considered only after projects are formalised and managed.

As shown in Figure 8.2, this viewpoint by domain is specified by identifying the parties taking part in the project.

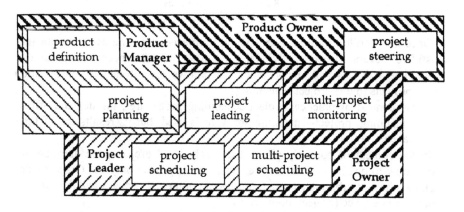

**Fig. 8.2** Parties taking part in the project

### 8.1.2.2   *Viewpoint of Those Deciding to Apply Some EUREX Techniques*

#### *The Sequence of Domains*

This sequence of domains (see Figure 8.3) represents (from the bottom upwards) the generic succession of questions asked by companies deciding to implement project mode in their organisations.

A frequently asked question relates to project scheduling and, more particularly, to walk-through of installing project-scheduling software: such software has been installed, but it is misused.

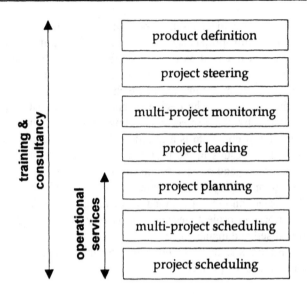

**Fig. 8.3** Sequence of domains

Once this hurdle has been overcome and project-scheduling activities are successful for several projects individually, the next request concerns integration of scheduling activities with a coherence that allows for substantial consolidation across projects (multi-project scheduling).

In the context of practical project scheduling procedures, the demand affects project planning: project-scheduling software is used, but its results are of little significance.

In the context of correctly planned and scheduled projects, the question becomes how to qualify or measure the substance of project progress (project leading), then how to arbitrate among priorities of competing projects and the capitalisation of experience (project monitoring).

Subsequently, requests coming from the Product Owner are aimed at determining if the result of the project underway is still adequate, taking account of an opportunity which was either refined, or has evolved.

Lastly, the commercial requests in the domain of product definition are at the meeting point of corporate culture and strategy. Does the change in question concern the project mode? Is this the right project? Is the product definition sufficiently clear and complete to be understood?

Companies playing the role for Project Owners start to ask questions in the domain of project scheduling.

Companies playing the role of Product Owner start to ask questions in the domain of project steering.

### Solutions

The solutions to the problems presented by the various domains are based on techniques. A technique is a form with its associated rules, a succession of arithmetic operations, or a procedure of installing software; that is, a technique is something you use. In project mode, operational personnel use techniques in their day-to-day processes.

A process is a series of elementary actions and interactions between individuals or groups which results in an identified outcome; a process is something which one does; a certain number of processes correspond to pre-established schemes: in this case, they can be formalised and transmitted.

For example, the mission of the project leader is to attain a defined result within a given time and defined budget. To do so, he must know the project progress status.

He calls his team together and checks on the progress status of each ongoing task (a process). At that time, each person in charge of a task formulates a technical progress report (a technique), and the project manager establishes the "earned value" (another technique).

Then, the project manager reports for the progress status in his project to the Project Owner (another process).

This process continues throughout the life of the project.

A frequent demand concerns operational needs that the people involved in a project do not meet satisfactorily. The improvement in answers is a question of using the processes. This is facilitated by:

- Transferring project mode techniques to users of the processes; and
- Accommodating differences in languages and cultures that exist between services or companies that must operate together on projects.

One answer may be to use a professional hired for the project to certify the processes used by the project. One or more such professionals may be used to implement the processes directly or to facilitate the use of the processes by others involved in the project. This second form is known as the consultancy.

Another answer involves acquisition of the necessary techniques within the organisation (training).

## 8.2  Adapt the Quality Level to Nature of Encountered Problems

Management often involves an observation that something went wrong in the past and the recognition that processes should be improved to avoid future occurrences of similar troubles.

Usually, improvement is based on a diagnosis of what went wrong. Then, a new target process is identified and a roadmap to achieve that – process improvement – is planned, decided and then implemented. Then successes and failures are analysed and addressed. Great! This is what this book is about.

Now, let's have another glance at the issue. Process improvement has been triggered by a problem in a project or with a client (internal or external). Implicit is the assumption that, prior to the particular project or client, all was well, or at least, all was acceptable. And then, suddenly from our perspective, problems appeared. Was it really all that sudden?

Considering several organisation models (like CMM or ISO-SPICE), here is a viewpoint on why things worked reasonably well before the problem occurred that triggered Process Improvement decision.

*Level 1(ad hoc):* we were previously successful because we had the right people at the right position. Then, my best justification is the resume of the key people of my projects.

*Level 2 (repeatable):* we were previously successful because we implemented similar projects so many times that we know our niche business. Then, my best justification is my reference list.

*Level 3 (defined):* we were previously successful because our process is defined (and written down) and we have objective ways to ensure quality. My best justification is then to show my quality manual or my ISO 9000 certificate.

*Level 4 (managed):* we were previously successful because our defined process is managed from measurements; consequently, we can prove it is managed. My best justification is then to show evidence from actual statistics.

*Level 5 (optimised):* we were previously successful because our defined and measured process was the one most compliant with the environment requirements. My best justification is then to show evidence that if we were not successful, then no risk analysis could have helped.

In theory, perfection within what is humanly achievable is met at level 5.

The best way to reach level 5 is to go through each of the intermediate levels, starting from one's current level. Thus, it makes sense to assess first which level one is in, and then to target the next level with appropriate process improvement actions.

In many cases, for example, a level 1 organisation attempts to implement metrics. Successful people are asked to put into practice such and such measurements. When problems crop up, they have the feeling of being overloaded. They feel the need for competent colleagues, not measurements that don't solve problems. Rejection, whether overt or covert, is observed and the technique (and associated tools) is considered inadequate. Introduction of function points failed in a number of organisations, not because function points are bad, but probably because it was not the right solution. It is clear. Level 4 is not next to level 1.

Organisation models like CMM and ISO-SPICE are not panaceas, but these models are founded on common sense observations that reflect life in organisations as it is.

Process Improvement has to be grounded in reality: best practice is to get an assessment first. Then, and only then, determine the next step.

For the vast majority of software development organisations, it is a long road to level 5. It may be a problem to achieve results quickly.

Then the question is value for the organisation: going to next step is not necessarily the best thing to do. Often, the best decision is to stay at the same level and strengthen it. For example, a company that is level 3, but which has problems, need not of necessity move to level 4. It might be more advantageous to redefine its processes (at least some of them), to improve them, but to remain at level 3. In the future, the situation may change, but the key is working within the constraints of one's organisation.

Compliance with the constraints of one's environment is the most important factor governing a process improvement decision. In other words, what makes the clients happy (whether inside or outside the company)?

In some cases, it might be the feeling they have the right person in front of them. Flexibility is the key to success. Only then should recruitment or level 5 be the focus.

Using a scale (from 1 to 5, as introduced above), what is the most appropriate level for an organisation? Ideally, he answer is level 5, but meeting this target might take too long and require too much effort, and might ultimately result in deterioration rather than improvement. This does not mean that targeting higher levels is wrong in general; it simply means that it is not necessarily the right solution at a given point in time.

Back to the Process Improvement trigger, the question is usually: "why did we fail?", when it could be extended to "why were we successful before we had a problem?". Where should the organisation be in the first place?

The answers to these questions will be found by studying the results of an assessment. Such results can be used to quantify the value and the cost of a process change.

A good recommendation is to promote changes that have more value than cost!

# Part III

# Process Improvement Experiments

# 9 Table of PIEs

Table 9.1 below lists each of the PIEs considered as part of the EUREX taxonomy within the problem domain of Project Management, Estimation and Life Cycle Support.

**Table 9.1** Table of PIEs

| Project No | Year of CfP | Acronym | Project Partners | Country |
|---|---|---|---|---|
| 21511 | 1995 | APPLY | VERILOG | F |
| 21545 | 1995 | BESTMM | HYPTIQUE | F |
| 21610 | 1995 | CARERRAS | BRITISH RAIL BUSINESS SYSTEMS | UK |
| 10327 | 1993 | CATALYST | Technisystems Ltd | GR |
| 10327 | 1993 | CATALYST | ROLLS-ROYCE AND ASSOCIATES LTD | UK |
| 23962 | 1996 | COCOSPIE | PHILOTECH GmbH | D |
| 10361 | 1993 | CSSC | AEG HAUSGERAETE AG | D |
| 21265 | 1995 | DATM-RV | FAME COMPUTERS Ltd | UK |
| 23699 | 1996 | DECO | ENGINEERING INGEGNERIA INFOR-MATICA S.p.A. | I |
| 21593 | 1995 | DIGIDOC | DIGIANSWER A/S | DK |
| 10024 | 1993 | EMS | VOEST ALPINE STAHL LINZ GMBH | A |
| 10476 | 1993 | ENG-SODEPRO | ENGINEERING-INGEGNERIA INFOR-MATICA S.p.A. | I |
| 21569 | 1995 | ESTEX | COMPUTER RESOURCES INTERNA-TIONAL A/S | DK |
| 10760 | 1993 | FAME | FIRST INFORMATICS S.A. | GR |
| 21622 | 1995 | FAMPIX | FEGS Ltd | UK |
| 21628 | 1995 | IMPACT | PRO DV Software GmbH | D |
| 23780 | 1996 | IMPOSE | MENTE SYSTEMUTVIKLING AS | N |
| 21733 | 1995 | INCOME | FINSIEL S.p.A. | I |
| 24085 | 1996 | INTRASUP-PORT | ICL Data Oy | SF |
| 10189 | 1993 | IPTPM | MATRA MARCONI SPACE | F |
| 10482 | 1993 | IQASP | LABEIN | E |
| 10482 | 1993 | IQASP | B.Y.G. SYSTEMS LTD | UK |
| 10549 | 1993 | MARITA | ABB ROBOTICS PRODUCTS AB | S |

| Project No | Year of CfP | Acronym | Project Partners | Country |
|---|---|---|---|---|
| 24287 | 1996 | MASLYD | I.C.E. COMPUTER SERVICES Ltd | IRL |
| 21476 | 1995 | MBM | ALENIA un' Azienda Finmeccania | I |
| 21294 | 1995 | MEFISTO | SOFTWARE ENGINEERING CENTRE DEFENCE RESEARCH AGENCY | UK |
| 21244 | 1995 | MIDAS | S.I.A. S.p.A. | I |
| 21443 | 1995 | MOOD | PARALLAX GROUP plc | UK |
| 23819 | 1996 | MOODS | OPENLAKE | I |
| 10995 | 1993 | ODAGUI | VTKK REGIONAL GOVERNMENT SYSTEMS LTD | SF |
| 10738 | 1993 | OPROB | MOTOMAN ROBOTICS AB | S |
| 24065 | 1996 | PCS | CLOCKWORKS MULTIMEDIA | IRL |
| 24158 | 1996 | PERSPI | COMPUTER LOGIC S.A. | GR |
| 23825 | 1996 | PIBOP | INTRACOM S.A. | GR |
| 10836 | 1993 | PRAMIS | LABEIN | E |
| 10836 | 1993 | PRAMIS | CCL | UK |
| 21167 | 1995 | PRIDE | BRÜEL & KJAER A/S | DK |
| 23795 | 1996 | PROMASYS | GONVARRI INDUSTRIAL S.A. | E |
| 24149 | 1996 | PROMISED | CSTB | F |
| 10616 | 1993 | PROMM | IRISH LIFE ASSURANCE PLC | IRL |
| 21513 | 1995 | REPRO | PROVIDA ASA | N |
| 10147 | 1993 | SCERA | NESTE OIL | SF |
| 23838 | 1996 | SELDOM | THERA S.p.A. | I |
| 10218 | 1993 | SMETOSQA | INFOGEA SRL | I |
| 21799 | 1995 | SPIRIT | BAAN COMPANY N.V. | NL |
| 10665 | 1993 | TIKE | MINISTRY OF AGRICULTURE AND FORESTRY / INFORMATION CENTRE TIKE | SF |
| 24091 | 1996 | TOPSPIN | TEDOPRES INTERNATIONAL B.V. | NL |

# 10 Summaries of PIE Reports

## 10.1 ALCAST 10146

### Implementation of an Automated Life-Cycle Approach to Software Testing in the Finance and Insurance Sector

The Automated Life Cycle Approach to Software Testing (ALCAST) project aimed to improve manual testing practices and then automate them in two finance/insurance sector organisations. The ALCAST consortium consisted of three companies; the Voluntary Health Insurance Board (VHI), Quay Financial Software (QFS) and Quality Software Engineering Technologies (Q·SET). The main interest groups for this project are companies who test software as part of their product development life cycle, and those who need to automate the process or parts of it, using tools.

The ALCAST project ran from January 1994 until June 1995. During Phase 1, software testing practices in both companies were first assessed against current best practice in the industry. Having identified key areas for improvement, the V Model was implemented as a process framework and then further enhanced using the Systematic Test and Evaluation Process (STEP) methodology.

In Phase 2 of the project, the VHI piloted an on-line test environment with automated defect tracking and change management. In QFS, support for STEP was included in their existing corporate information system and automation of both regression testing and static analysis took place. The main lessons learned were as follows:

- Specific ALCAST lessons:
- Testing should be involved at the project requirements stage.
- The STEP methodology has proved effective when tailored for individual company needs.
- Unit testing pays, but overheads and administration should be kept to a minimum.
- Test automation is beneficial but has a significant learning curve.
- Metrics should be kept simple and usable.
- Training for best practices is essential to ensure the success of a company wide implementation.
- General Project Management lessons:

- Improvement must be managed as a mainstream project in a company, with equal or higher priority than core business projects.
- Expertise in tools and automation should be gathered as a company asset into teams and used as a resource on projects.
- The initial assessment in the cycle of Assess, Improve and Measure is critical for gauging the success of the Project.

The next actions will be to run an end of project dissemination event in Ireland (estimated 150 companies attending) and distribute this report in booklet form to Q·SET customers (>7000).

The project was regarded as a success in all 3 companies and plans are in place for company wide implementation.

Members of the ALCAST Project gratefully acknowledge the moral support and financial help provided by the ESSI Group at the European Commission without which ALCAST would not have happened.

## 10.2   AMIGO 21222

## Achievements of Software Maintenance Improvement Goals

The objective of AMIGO has been to improve the organisation of the SW Maintenance process at ELIOP in a systematic way in order to:

- Improve its effectiveness
- Track the problems and corrective actions efficiently and according to quality standards
- Introduce some defect prevention activities
- Provide related quality metrics
- Increase the level of satisfaction of the involved people.

This Process Improvement Experiment (PIE) has been carried out by ELIOP as the single contractor, with the financial support of the European Commission, within the framework of the European Systems and Software Initiative (ESSI).

ELIOP SA is a Spanish company with 100 employees, 30 of them directly involved in SW engineering. Its main activity is the delivery of Industrial Control Systems, including software for standard computers or embedded into microprocessor-based in-house manufactured equipment. Such systems require real time, continuous operation, and often they are controlling critical industrial processes. Software is a very important part of the added value of ELIOP products.

The work performed started setting-up the project organisation, performing a general approach study, and selecting the organisational and process changes to be experienced in the project context. Appropriate metrics and tools were identified and selected. A precise definition of the experiments was done and selected tools were installed and set-up. In the second half of the project, after doing the needed training activities, defined experiments were put into practice. Final stages of the project include a review of the procedures and the evaluation of results of the experiments. Some of the improvements were selected to be introduced as regular practices in the company and a plan was set-up to do so.

Most significant lessons learned from the project are the following ones:

- The efforts devoted to maintenance are very distributed in different tasks, and the causes of the software defects are also very spread, so it is not feasible to achieve outstanding improvements acting only on very specific aspects of the maintenance process.
- A positive Return on Investment has been demonstrated for most of the improvements experienced.
- Object oriented code using C++ language raises some important maintenance problems. It is very convenient introducing direct/reverse design tools early in the life cycle, and starting using them firstly for direct design.
- The experiment has confirmed an initial negative consideration from the software engineers towards the maintenance work. Some improvements introduced in the management of software defects has reached an outstanding acceptance from the involved people.

## 10.3   APPLY 21511

### Amplified Process Performance Layout

VERILOG is a manufacturer of software and system engineering tools. VERILOG was looking for an improvement of its internal practices to deliver better products to its customers and for an increase of its experience to help external organisations to plan and implement its technologies. The APPLY project is the experiment of the combined application of recommendations coming from a global Process Improvement Program initiated after a CMM self assessment. The main objective of APPLY was to implement the recommendations on a real size project in order to validate them and to obtain a quantitative project profile (cost break down and benefits) to facilitate internal and external replication.

The main achievement of APPLY are:

- Definition of a Project Control Panel capturing metrics on process performance, quality of the final product.
- Implementation of new practices supported by tools in the areas of:
  - Requirements Management.
  - Project Planning and Tracking.
  - Configuration Management.

• Test and Validation.

APPLY results are:

- A better project control:
  - Initial budget respected,
  - delivery time managed within a 5% window (but the initial date is not respected).
- A higher reliability of the final product:
  - Remaining bugs are divided by 2 for the same test effort

Economical consequences have to be evaluated on market side rather than on the internal productivity benefits. For instance, VERILOG has had 40% product sales growth and an increase of maintenance contract renewal.

The description of this experiment could give to other organisations ideas and facts in order to replicate such improvement.

This work has been financed by the European Commission as part of the ESSI program.

## 10.4    ARETES 24148

### Application of Reliability Engineering in Testing During Software Localisation

The ARETES project aimed at the application of the Software Reliability Engineering methodology into the testing performed during the software localisation process. It is funded by the Commission of the European Communities (CEC) as an Application Experiment under the ESSI programme: European System and Software Initiative. The ESSI goal is to promote improvements in Software Development processes, in order to achieve greater efficiency, higher quality and increased economy.

Archetypon introduced in ARETES the use of Software Reliability Techniques in order to evaluate the benefits of it, during the testing of localised products. According to this initiative a traditional software testing baseline project was selected and held in Archetypon. A new approach was applied on parts of the project's life cycle and the results were recorded and compared to the results of the traditional testing process. The use of Software Reliability Engineering in Testing has shown important results such as:

- Increase in testing productivity
- Earlier failure detection of severe failures
- Reduction of customer reported problems
- Identification of the areas of the Software that need increased testing effort.
- Effective Management of the testing resources and improvement of the resulting reliability of the application.

- Predict the level of the Reliability of the Software earlier than the ending date of the testing process.

The key lessons learned from this experiment can be summarised as follows:

- Development of an Operational Profile proved to be the most difficult and time-consuming tasks.
- Special care should be given to the data collection since this will have great impact in the accuracy of the measurements and the results
- Training of the people involved in SRE projects is very important for the success of the experiment
- SRE is applicable to large-scale projects in order to absorb the overhead introduced from the initial phases of the project.

The ARETES experiment provided enough quantitative data that made feasible a comparison of this approach with the traditional approach followed. The evaluation of this new approach's usability concluded that the use of Software Reliability techniques is beneficial in testing a product and providing critical results. Nevertheless, the application of such techniques is more effective in large-scale projects, due to the overhead that appears in the early stages of the application of such techniques.

All the members of the ARETES Project gratefully acknowledge the moral support and financial help provided by the ESSI Group at the European Commission, without which ARETES would not have taken place.

## 10.5    AUTOMA 10564

### Automated Corrective and Evolutionary Maintenance for Database Intensive Application Products

The AUTOMA experiment has concerned the improvement of maintenance activities for complex data management applications, through the formalisation and automation of

- requirements management
- configuration management
- regression testing.

The project has selected the appropriate tools and technologies, and has used them to build two complementary experiment scenarios, based on the maintenance activities of two project groups (one for each partner).

The project has been fully successful in the experimentation of Configuration Management and Requirements management.

In the first case, the whole maintenance line of a complex system has been put under fully automated control, developing (on top of the selected tool) a CM environment and related procedures capable of ensuring full control while avoiding any extra effort for the maintenance teams (actually contributing to improve the overall efficiency).

On the second aspect, the specifications of another system (in continuous evolution due to changing and increasing user requirements) have been formalised and are now under tool-supported control.

The results obtained on testing shows some problem; at the beginning, more resistance has been experienced on these aspects by the development teams, despite the reduced involvement requested (the preparation of test procedures was performed by dedicated resources), due to the difficulties of showing the advantages of the approach.

The preparation phase has been however successful, and allowed to derive interesting lessons on how to extract and formalise the functional knowledge required to prepare good, effective functional tests.

Once an initial set of automated test procedures has been prepared, its exploitation suffered problems related to the high level of changes that the two systems are still experiencing from one release to the other; this has prevented, till now, a real deployment of automated testing on one of the two systems, while a partial automated testing approach is currently operational for the other.

Despite these difficulties, however, the need to formalise test procedures has injected a radical organisational change in the two maintenance teams, that now handle testing-related activities in a quite better way. This is demonstrated by the comparison of the process assessments conducted before and after the experiment.

## 10.6   BESTMM 21545

### Methods and tools to improve software quality for multimedia products

BESTMM is a project dedicated to best practice in multimedia production, funded and supported by the EEC. Although the project is initiated by the objective of software quality improvement, the topic covers the larger field of optimisation of the overall process of multimedia production, in terms of methods and tools.

These products are combining media (text, still and moving pictures, sound) with software in a sophisticated and constantly moving technological environment.

Everybody involved in the quickly growing community of multimedia professionals should be interested in the conclusions of this experimentation : publishers will understand better the implications of their intentions on the design and production process, financial partners will understand better the use of their investments, but the main objective of this project is to offer to producers a methodology for the organisation, management and accomplishment the complex set of tasks that are necessary to produce multimedia titles.

In a first phase, after analysing the objectives of the experimentation, a general purpose model of staff structure and tasks organisation has been defined from previous experience. In a second phase, we have tested this model on our baseline project : the design and production of an edutainment CD-Rom, for children between 6 and 10 years old. This model is precisely described in this report and in the diagrams given in the annexes.

Multimedia production is a new industry in which creative and cultural activities are confronted to highly structured tasks of integration and software development. Clear formalisation of the objectives and of the technical and artistic guidelines is a condition to avoid endless prototyping. Keeping detailed trace of the production process is the condition to capitalise the know-how, for the benefit of future projects.

In its everyday practice, this effort of formalisation was not easy in a company like Hyptique where creativity prevails. The first concrete benefits are surprisingly in the commercial action, in which the evaluation of new propositions and the pedagogic effort to clients coming recently to multimedia has been significantly improved.

The completion of the experiment consists of a final analysis of the baseline project and the evaluation of the overall benefit from BESTMM on Hyptique's multimedia production.

## 10.7    CARERRAS 21610

### Case Study of Analysis and Re-engineering of Railway Resource Allocation Systems

CARERRAS is a Process Improvement Experiment to establish metrics, standards and processes to support re-engineering legacy systems. The experiment is being carried out by BR Business Systems(BRBS). The work has mainly been carried out by the PIE project manager and the re-engineering project manager.

Prior to the experiment, BRBS's Quality Management System provided support for standard projects with technically based metrics. The experiment is to produce additional processes for re-engineering projects together with process based metrics.

The experiment covered 4 project stages, analysis, development, testing and installation along with the overall project management.

The main results and findings are :

The attempted technical re-engineering did not prove successful due both to technical problems and the customers business changing during the lifetime of the experiment. On the reporting of this change the commission carried out a project review to ensure that the project would still fulfil the purpose for which it was chosen and funding allocated. Additionally the review recommended extending the project timescales but not the effort for the PIE to take account of the delays incurred in the baseline project to allow proper completion of the experiment after baseline project implementation. The need for the experiment to focus on the means of re-engineering taking into account business change made it all the more worthwhile.

Customers are very supportive of the move to re-engineer their legacy systems based on the logical re-engineering model. This has resulted in a 25% increase in customers and a 5 fold increase in revenue from this customer base to fund the ongoing re-engineering. This is due to the re-engineering process underwriting BRBS's long term plans for the customers business area, planning for and supporting business change, the development of a controlled process and a recognition of the business, its pressures and its changing requirements.

The development structure proposed in the experiment was introduced on the baseline project and has successfully been reused on projects in other business areas within BRBS. This has allowed the Development phase to be very similar to that in standard lifecycle developments with a different overlying organisation and technical structure including the breakdown of large projects into smaller ones with their inherent decrease in risks..

The overall expected divergences from the standard lifecycle have come at the start of the project, in the analysis phase, rather than in the development phase, as originally predicted.

As a result of the experiment, we have a recommended process for analysis and development for re-engineering projects. We also have metrics for estimating the analysis stage of future re-engineering projects

The experiments assumptions that testing and implementation metrics for re-engineering projects would now follow those already understood for project development, have proved correct. The major difference, found in implementation, being the need to plan for and carry out culture change, data cleansing and conversion from the old systems. This has resulted in higher than normal implementation costs for the baseline project.

A second re-engineering project has already been started using the results of this experiment.

## 10.8   CASSIOPEE 21522

### Improving Methodologies for Efficiently Designing Decision Support Software for Aircraft Maintenance

CASSIOPEE is the name for a project which has been funded from January 2 1996 to May 2 1997 by the European Commission as part of the ESSI software best practice initiative. The project aims at improving the company's ability to design and implement software systems for aircraft engine maintenance using case based reasoning and knowledge discovery techniques. Our goals are to :

- control the development of diagnostic software in terms of costs and delays
- control the maintenance of the software
- assure the quality of the software system during its whole life cycle

This project should be of particular interest to those communities who are already using or developing systems based on knowledge discovery or those who are involved in maintenance activities of complex technical systems where human experience is essential and who wish to improve them by developing such systems.

The main results of the project were the obtaining of a methodology ruling the development process of diagnostic systems and its application to one engine type. This includes the development of current engine failure models which are necessary to the system, the definition and setting up of an organisation dedicated to collecting quality cases. The whole development cycle has been undertaken 1,5 times, since the methodology was applied to two distinct engine types.

The work achieved has helped us improve the process by which we develop quality decision support software. Fewer cases but of higher quality and an organisation for case collection and quality control are key indicators for the efficiency of the implemented methodology. This yields to higher accuracy on the average consultation (83% precision instead of a maximum of 20% prior to the experiment) and to a reduction of the cycle and cost of development by a factor of 2. For 6 systems on all our engines, this represents a saving of K$600 of cash flow (42% gain) on the development cost. It also moves forward by two and a half years the break even point for our global business plan for case based diagnostic software.


# 10.9    CATALYST 10327

## Use of CommonKADS Methodology in Knowledge Based System Development

This report covers the experiences of ESSI project 10327 – Catalyst. Catalyst concerns the uptake of the CommonKADS method in the development of KBS (Knowledge Based Systems). Two users were involved in the adoption of the methods: RRA (Rolls-Royce and Associates Ltd) (UK) and OM (Oceanking Maritime) (GR). This work would not have been possible without the funding and support provided by the European Commission.

The report gives a background to the project and companies involved, but concentrates on the main lessons learned. These are in three main areas: general lessons regarding CommonKADS, expertise modelling and project management. The report ends with some conclusions and recommendations. These are targeted at KBS developers and the CommonKADS community, including tool vendors.

The experiment finds that CommonKADS is a large method which requires a substantial amount of learning and tailoring for specific use. RRA have found that the effort involved in customising the methods has been worthwhile, but recommends that other organisations on limited budgets adopt the methods piecemeal and more pragmatically than the CommonKADS theory suggests. The risk-driven project management activities have been scoped and now form part of RRA's KBS procedures. These project management techniques can easily be adapted for any project – KBS, software or other.

OM found that CommonKADS improved their project management procedures. On the other hand, the use of CommonKADS proved to have marginal applicability to small scale projects, because of the resulting substantial overhead.

The report will be of interest to all KBS developers (particularly those interested in formalising the development approach), the CommonKADS community, project managers with an interest in risk project management and vendors of CommonKADS modelling tools.

## 10.10   CMEX 21568

## Configuration Management Experiment

This experiment aims to improve the efficiency in a software development department by introducing a new and advanced configuration management system. The aim of the experiment is to reduce the number of error reports by 10% and the time-to-market by 5%.

The experiment was done in the development department of Sysdeco GIS AS in Norway, developing software for the mapping industry or GIS sector (Geographic Information Systems).

The experiment shows significant better results than originally aimed for. The errors have been reduced by 35,7% and the development effort has increased by 22%. The latter has contributed to bring the new products quicker to the market. The identified process improvement is not just a result of introducing a new system, but a result of many additional factors as general process improvement, product maturity and a focus on new development, to mention the most important.

Apart from the result above, the key lessons from the experiment have been:

- To introduce the new configuration tool, ClearCase, was more difficult than anticipated. Careful planning and experimenting took more time than planned and caused more problems for the developers than expected.
- Too little training using the new system made the introduction of the system difficult.

- Well-established routines for handling errors and a well-experienced development group significantly contributed the success of the experiment.
- Relevant background data to measure the improvement was harder to collect than anticipated. It took more time and required also more effort to analyse than expected.
- The management of the project has gained valuable experience in how to collect and analyse data regarding process improvement. New ideas for further improvements have been identified.

The success of the experiment makes it evident to continue to use the new system in our development and maintenance of our products. Further improvements can and will be done. We have also identified new areas for improvements and we plan to do a similar experiment introducing automatic testing tools.

This experiment is relevant for SMBs planning to introduce new tools in their development department, especially configuration management tools. The European Commission through the ESSI/PIE program with project # 21.568 has financially supported this project.


## 10.11   COMPRO 21573

### Component and Object Oriented Maturing Development Process Through Reuse Organisation

DI Systemer AS develops and supplies economy management systems in the fields of accounting, orders/invoices and salaries to small businesses in Norway. DI Systemer AS has a total of 24 employees, of whom 7 work in the development department.

The main objectives of COMPRO were: to implement development procedures and roles where reuse is an important element, to build libraries of reusable components and hence improve quality, increase productivity and reduce time-to-market. The plan was to reach maturity level 2 (and parts of level 3) of RMM – the "Reuse Maturity Level" (akin to the well known CMM – Capability Maturity Model).

Various technical and organisational problems arose in the course of the project, leading to delays and difficulties. It became clear that it would not be possible to carry out all of the work of the project as planned, and so it was decided (in consultation with the commission) that it would be best to terminate the project.

The premature termination of the project meant that not all of the objectives of the project were achieved in full. Despite this, the project was useful and some important lessons were learned. These were useful to our own organisation and – we hope – may be of assistance to other organisations considering similar process improvements.

Development procedures and roles were introduced, and led to benefits within the organisation.

A reuse oriented approach to software development was introduced, and some reusable components were produced. Our general conclusion is that this work showed some promise – but that the benefits of reuse remain so far unproven.

We worked at a detailed level with RMM, analysing the requirements imposed by RMM and drawing conclusions regarding the consequences for our organisation. We did some work towards implementing steps to take account of this, but our general conclusion is that RMM in its current form is not suitable for application in an organisation as small as ours.

In the course of the project, object-oriented programming techniques were introduced, together with a number of advanced tools. These will continue to be used.

All in all, the project has had a positive impact within our company. Awareness of the importance of process improvement, quality assurance and reuse has increased considerably. Specific skills have been acquired and applied, and the organisation is more mature and effective than at the start of the project.

## 10.12   CONFITEST 24362

### Creating a Solid Configuration and Test-Management Infrastructure to Improve the Team Development of Critical Software Systems

The experiment could only be carried out with the financial support of the Commission, in the specific programme for research and technological development in the field of information technologies.

TeSSA Software NV is a developer of critical software systems for different markets. The baseline Project is a typical TeSSA Software NV product, situated in the market of paypoints.

The experiment, situated in the domain of configuration- and test-management, has contributed to the aim of being a software production house that delivers quality systems in time.

### Project Goals

By implementing the software control management the project manager can optimise the development process, in concrete terms:

- Cost reduction (10 - 15 %)
- Elimination of errors in an early phase of the process (1 in stead of 10)
- Quality improvement of delivered programmes.
- Reliability increase of installed programmes.

- And last but not least, acceleration of the definite product delivery (about 10%).

Reaching these goals indirectly results in a better work-atmosphere for programmers, analysts, project managers and management.

This experiment will also be part of the efforts, TeSSA Software NV is making to produce a quality manual and obtain ISO9000 certification (Specially ISO 12207).

## Work Done

A quality manager was indicated and an internal base-reference report is written, to situate problems and costs. The global IT company strategy was defined and the specific requirements of this PIE are exactly defined to fit in this strategy. In the running of this PIE we had to change the global plan a few times. Looking for other existing models we found SPIRE (ESSI Project 21419) promoting CMM and BootCheck, 2 very interesting projects, giving a wider frame for the global plan.

The strategic choice between the different tools is part of this PIE and the choice has been made:

- Version control system and configuration management : PVCS
- Testtool : SQA Teamtest

One employee was trained in PVCS, another one in SQA Teamtest. Both products are installed, we got consultancy on both products and a global session on test-methods was given to everyone in the company. This was an important session to convince every one of the strategic choices.

In both domains the first procedures were implemented.

## Results

At the end of the experiment, every employee agrees that quality and reliability of the software development process is improved significantly. First figures give a global improvement of 5%. This is less then expected (7 à 10%), but we believe that the positive influence in productivity and reliability will become more and more visible in the next years.

The confidence in this experiment certainly helps to get a better working atmosphere.

The responses of the customers prove the confidence in the strategy of our company, working hard on the improvement of our internal processes and they see the first results of the new working methods.

## Future Actions

Now the procedures are consolidated and standardised to support the development cycle internally on the same LAN, the next step will be to extend the procedures to also support external employees.

With the help of our internal organisation with Lotus Notes Applications, the proceedings and the procedures are nowadays continuously internally disseminated.

At this moment we're still looking for opportunities to disseminate our knowledge externally.

## 10.13   CONTE 10505

### Continuous Improvement in Software Production at Eritel

The CONTE project is the Eritel's answer to a generalised worry in the Software Community: development of better software, with higher quality and productivity, is required. How can an Organisation face this improvement requirement?, which are the strategies to follow?, what elements can help the managers to improve the development process? and, how can the Organisations know the progress achieved?. Aiming to answer these and other related questions, the CONTE project has been designed.

Thus, the main objective of this project was to improve the software development and management process in order to decrease costs and achieve higher quality systems, as well as to disseminate the results achieved to a wider community.

This solution was framed in a Best Practice Model that comprises all the software production environment aspects considered as key points to obtain a significant improvement in the development process at Eritel. These issues have been: project estimation and productivity; process management; technological evolution; metrics application; human and project support and customer satisfaction. The experience obtained through CONTE and this model should serve to establish the basis of the continuous process improvement at the entire company.

The work done to achieve this goal has consisted in a first assessment of the situation in which some weaknesses were detected, mainly related to: the necessity of more reliable project estimation and objective measures of productivity and quality; the need for a more flexible production model allowing higher adaptation to different project features and the need to incorporate to the software practices new development technologies approaches.

As main results of this experiment, it can be mentioned the improvement of existing Eritel components like the *Process Model*, the *Project Management system* and the *Configuration Management system*. Also some new components oriented to the continuous process improvement have been added, like: put in practice a *Metrics Program*; the design and experimentation of a *Process Assessment Method* and a *Customer Satisfaction Assessment Method*, and finally an effective basis to make evolve the Eritel's quality and production environment (Q-MEIN).

Initial definition of these components was refined after having tested them trough several projects, in accordance to two actuation lines defined: one is the

Action Plan, which includes general actions for improving and collecting metrics from a number of projects as large as possible, and the other one is to concentrate our effort in the experimentation of the process improvement in a few number of projects.

A significant result of CONTE project has been the better knowledge achieved about our software production process, in terms of quality and productivity indicators, as well as how to achieve a continuous process improvement as a systematic and step by step process. From the analysis of the results collected, some improvement actions have been arisen, some of them for specific projects and other ones for the entire company.

The most important next proposed actions are to generalise reuse of software products to the entire company, as well as to follow on the line of having more indicators of the production process.

This experimentation and its results should be of interest for any software house, or IT departments willing to increase the quality and effectiveness of their software development process. Also, people who want to adopt or experiment with metrics would take some advantage from this project.

This experiment has been carried out by Eritel in the framework of the Community Research Programme with a financial contribution by the European Commission.

## 10.14  DATM-RV 21265

### Determination of Appropriate Tools and Methodology as Applied to a Combined RAD-V Life Cycle

This report is the summary of the findings and results from ESSI experiment 21265 DATM-RV, Determination of Appropriate Tools and Methodology for a combined Rad-"V" life cycle. The business motivation behind the project was to enable Fame Computers Ltd to be able to meet the increasing demands of our customers to deliver products to market faster, at reduced cost and ever increasing quality. An assessment was made of our ISO9001 certified development processes, via our internal audit programme, to understand where key processes or tools required improvement in order to meet these objectives of efficiency and effectiveness. Whilst being compliant to international quality standards there is always potential for improvement and the following common process characteristics were assessed as being candidates for a series of mini improvement experiments to be performed through the funding of the ESSI programme.

- Projects employed only a standard "V" life cycle and made no use of iterative or rapid development life cycles and supporting tools where potentially these could efficiently reduce cycle time or improve the quality of the requirements capture process

- Limited use of CASE tools were used to support systems analysis. This was restricted to classical database entity relationship analysis with little potential for efficient forward engineering into subsequent project phases.
- Limited use of Object Oriented analysis and design methods or tools to support existing Object Oriented implementation using conventional 3GL (C++) environments, compromising the quality and continuity of the analysis, design and implementation life cycle.
- Unit testing was performed by individual programmers but not formally specified to ensure rigour or analysed for effectiveness with coverage tools, thus diluting the effect of a valuable early stage of verification and validation.
- System testing was a textual scripting process that was manually executed. With any test cycle repetition this process would become increasingly inefficient, therefore by limiting repetition to save time the potential effectiveness of this process for finding system errors was not sufficiently exploited.
- The Quality Management System was manually implemented with a manual document control system that reduced the potential effectiveness of the quality practices and reuse of existing documentation because of inadequate and inefficient access to documentary and intellectual assets within the business.

By applying a range of mini experiments to improve these processes it was intended that the business goals of productivity and quality would be more readily achieved. Figure 10.1 illustrates the results of some of the experiments where productivity and return on investment have been possible to measure.

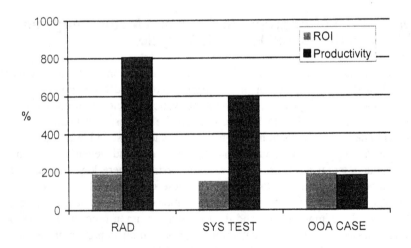

**Fig. 10.1** Return On Investment and productivity for selected experiments

The results of the experiments are:

- Projects can now employ a RAD life cycle with 4GL tools providing up to 709% productivity gains with an improved requirements capture and maintenance process.
- CASE tools are now available to support object oriented analysis providing productivity gains of 85% over previous methods, with improvement in quality of analysis due to formal analysis methods
- Object Oriented analysis and design methods that show promise of high quality reusable components developed to better meet requirements by the use of an iterative life cycle.
- Rigorous Unit testing that has improved the process to assure the quality of receipt of third party developed software.
- System testing techniques that have provided a 600% cost reduction by detecting errors earlier in the development life cycle, with the potential for cost reduction and increased effectiveness by automation of test repetition.
- An on-line Quality Management System that has reduced asset management costs by 68% and increased the availability of quality procedures and reusable documentary assets across the company. A 0.4% increase in productivity per employee through better practice or document reuse would see the system cost paid back within one year

From these results the ESSI experiment has been a success and has contributed to achieving the overall business objectives of improved productivity and quality of our processes and products.

## 10.15  DSP-ACTION 23696

### Improving DSP Software Documentation Process to Promote Reuse

The efforts invested in the development of digital signal processing software are increasing dramatically, especially in telecommunication applications. Design of optimised mathematical algorithms has dominated research and product development, but as the size of software has grown, a need for improved software development practices has emerged. DSP-ACTION is a joint-project of Nokia Mobile Phones (NMP) and Finnish Technical Research Centre/VTT Electronics. The project was funded by the European Union under the ESSI program. The objective of this process improvement experiment was to improve DSP software development process in order to promote reuse of every level of design documentation. The experiment was piloted in a real product development project aiming at solving practical problems in everyday design and development work in industry. Effective review practice was introduced by defining elements of DSP software quality after analysing the customer needs of both forthcoming and current projects. Current revision management system was hierarchically restructured to intuitively reflect every domain of the pilot project's DSP software. Creation and collection of process documents into a single location founded a base for continuous process improvement. The expected impact of the experiment was faster cycles of high-quality product development with the use of collective base of design level experience. Quantitative measurements were used to guide current and future process development activities.

The experiment indicated that DSP software process can be improved using systematic approach and taking into consideration practical needs of the pilot project. Measurements also indicated significant reusability improvements in many aspects compared to the previous situation. We believe that efforts required for this kind of process improvement are biggest in the beginning, but after the organisation has gained experience on process improvement less effort is required to continue with next steps of process improvement. Our next steps will include continuation of the follow-up with most interesting metrics, gaining more experiences from project, and replicating proven best practices in other DSP software development projects.

## 10.16   ENGMEAS 21162

## Introduction of Effective Metrics for Software Products in a Custom Software Development Environment

Measurement is an integral part of total quality management and process improvement strategies. We measure to understand and improve our processes. A software measurement programme allows organisations to improve their understanding of their development and support processes, leading to rational, planned improvements. Measurement programs also provide organisations with the ability to prioritise and concentrate their efforts on areas needing the greatest improvements.

Motivated by such considerations, the ENG-MEAS Process Improvement Experiment – conducted by Engineering Ingegneria Informatica S.p.A with the support of the Commission of the European Communities within the European Software and Systems Initiative (ESSI) – dealt with the definition of a company wide software metrics database. The project started in January 1996 and ended in June 1997, lasting 18 months.

As a large Italian software house, Engineering Ingegneria Informatica S.p.A. experiments all problems typical of software organisations involved in large turnkey projects for custom software products in rapidly evolving technological environments. Concerning this scenario, the definition and implementation of a measure programme was aimed to increase the company's capabilities in predicting and controlling software projects and in ensuring objective assessment of both the developed software and the software development process.

Since the most successful way to determine what we should measure is to tie the measurement program to our organisational goals and objectives, the PIE selected the "Goal-Question-Metric" (GQM) method for tying the measurements to the goals.

The experiment was intended to characterise the company's process productivity and defectiveness in terms of some technological, methodological, organisational and cultural factors, chosen for their relevance (i.e., that might have a significant effect, typically those that are not restricted to a small part of the lifecycle).

Main choices included:

- introduction of new software sizing techniques, based on Function Points analysis,
- systematic definition of the measurement plan through the GQM method,
- adoption of adequate statistical procedures for data analysis:
- a procedure for analysing unbalanced datasets that include many nominal and ordinal scale factors. It is adequate for obtaining company statistical baselines. In our context, a statistical baseline comprises the average values and variance of productivity or defect rates for projects developed by the company, allowing for the affect of significant variation factors,
- an anomaly detection analysis. We used it in identifying those projects that deviate significantly from other projects either by being extremely good or extremely bad.

## 10.17  ENG-SODEPRO 10476

### Experimentation of a new software development process, oriented to software quality

An approach to software quality requirements specification process and methods for software development projects control are shown. In addition, the experience gained in the experimentation performed is discussed.

The addressed technical objectives of the A.E. can be summarised in:

- Revision and enhancement of the company's structured methodology, named METHIS, which covers all phases of software development, in order to formally and clearly address not only the project's functional requirements but also the quality (non-functional) ones.
- Introduction of a set of process development indicators for controlling and monitoring software development process in detail and on a fixed (monthly) basis.

This in order to obtain the following business objectives:

- Capability to tailor the development activities to the quality requirements specific for each customer/project.
- To enhance the quality of the delivered software products, and to make visible its achievement to the user.
- To enhance productivity and costs control, through an earlier discovery and resolution of problems.

The adoption of this new approach is a key part of a continuous organisational revision process of the company, already certified compliant with the ISO 9001 standards.

The approach has been successfully experimented and two major organisational results can be underlined:

- the awareness by the technical staff of the software quality related issues and the implications on the development process;
- a better definition of the role of the Quality Assurance function and its more effective integration within the company's business mainstream.

On the other hand, it is not possible to fail to acknowledge that an higher tool support for the software quality requirements specification process is requested to reduce the implied overhead in effort.


## 10.18  ESTREMA 23724

### Estimation Improvement Based on Improved Requirements Management

Gruppo PRO's core business is information systems automation in medium and large industrial companies. We customise and install software products developed by ourselves and we provide assistance to the start up of the automated systems. In our projects, because of the incompleteness of the requirements and the lack of a common methodology, the accuracy of the initial estimates was low and unanticipated work used to creep in unmanaged. We analysed the available historical data about our projects' performance: 82 contracts were considered and we found out that in 79% of our bigger contracts we were over budget in a range from 110% to 150%.

In 1997 we launched ESTREMA, an eighteen months PIE (Process Improvement Experiment) meant to increase the reliability of our cost and schedule estimates and to reduce the percentage of unanticipated work by improving our requirements management capabilities, including control over the requirements changes.

The PIE started in March 1997 and requiring 543 person/ days internal effort and 48 persons days of third party assistance.

The main results of ESTREMA are:

- a common methodology to carry out one of our standard projects covering requirements, estimation and a standard project execution process
- an in-house developed estimation aid based on the phases and tasks identified in the common methodology
- a project tracking mechanism based on a projects performance database.

The benefits gained by our company are:

- a common methodology provides a framework of consistent and repeatable tasks that are to be carried out for all projects of similar characteristics
- more accurate estimates have been obtained by approaching the estimation task in a systematic way
- the utilisation of a consistent methodology has enabled better tracking from the project's outset
- the projects performance database allows us to compare progress across projects, therefore we can begin to develop an historic record of actual data to enable better estimates in the future.

Experimenting a measurement mechanism to assess improvement in estimating is difficult within a PIE; the time span of a ERP project is much longer and only tracking it until the end could give us the opportunity to measure the project performance against the initial estimates. For this reason we do not have definitive data about the precision improvement gained. However in ESTREMA we made an assessment on the basis of what emerged at the initial progress status checkpoints and our prediction is that a 50% improvement on accuracy in the most critical type of projects (large size projects) could show up even in the first iteration of the method.

Having reached a positive conclusion of ESTREMA we are now extending the new methodology to all the projects sharing the same process of the baseline project, which are the vast majority of our projects. In fact the new practices suit them already since they have been conceived with their process in mind. In the longer term we will also incorporate different types of projects.

## 10.19 EQISOMM 21397

### Effective and Quality Improving Software Maintenance Method

The project was about the implementation of a maintenance methodology, (phases, circuits and procedures) in two very different systems. One of them was a PROFit software product which had a very intensive evolution since start of the PIE. The other system was composed of two in house developed financial applications, without existing documentation and where the maintenance therefore depended very much on the maintenance staff. Both systems were in production at Banco Fomento Exterior (BFE).

The project objectives were:

- To free up the staff with more technical and business experience from maintenance.
- To provide a people independent maintenance process.
- To introduce a methodology, techniques and quality criteria in an area usually poorly systemised.
- To obtain the real maintenance costs and hence decide the most cost effective way forward.
- To enhance process and data structures so as to rectify maintenance "black holes".

The implementation gave very good results, even though it suffered a delay as a consequence of the resistance of specific people to leaving "their" applications in the first part of the project.

Later, the IT manager ordered the people to reduce their time on "their" applications, dedicating only 10 per cent of their time. The staff overreacted and left the applications totally and the productivity obviously decreased. In the October project tracking reports the situation was clearly identified and corrected. At the end of the project high level people had been almost totally substituted.

The implementation of a formal maintenance method was achieved, based on up to date documentation covering business processes to organic modules, which allowed the substitution of people in the planned timescales. Moreover, the register of system activities allowed the planning and management of the complete process, determining costs and locating where there was excessive maintenance.

For both projects the results were very positive,

- a net reduction of monthly maintenance costs of about 25%.
- a one year payback for the investment (in training and documentation).

For the maintenance of the software product it was also very important to free up people that could be dedicated to more sales type work and this was achieved. All the highly qualified technical people have been substituted and dedicated to sales support, the product now supports Year 2000 and the company in a good market position.

For the maintenance of the financial applications it has been decided to extend the method to more applications, because standardisation and cost reduction are strategic actions for BFE. Since October people from other applications have been joining the team to learn the methodology and together with other internal presentations, we can say that internal dissemination has been completed. For the next year there is a plan to spread the methodology to the whole department.

The main lessons learned during the experiment can be summarised as follows:

- The implementation of a new methodology is weakly supported until the people that have to use it can see and "feel" real progress. Metrics are very difficult to implement. Support of higher management is essential for both.
- To be competitive it is necessary to breakdown and categorise maintenance tasks in order to know which parts are important and which can be reduced.
- Changes in people's responsibilities must be carefully planned and management driven to achieve success.

## 10.20 FAME 10760

## Framework for Management and Design of Multimedia Applications in Education and Training

This report describes the FAME application experiment, an experiment which adapted and integrated state-of-the-art methodologies and tools in most phases of the development of an educational multimedia application in order to improve the software process. Specific goals of the experiment were to increase the product quality, reduce production duration and cost, apply more efficient monitoring and management processes, and improve quality assurance mechanisms. Furthermore, through several dissemination actions, the participants aimed at promoting their ability to exploit state-of-the-art software supports, enhance their credibility and improve the efficiency of respective software products and methodologies.

The experiment adapted and integrated these methodologies and tools during most phases of the development of a real application, the baseline experiment, emphasising requirement analysis and specification, design, quality assurance, metrics, review and evaluation. A small scale experiment adapted carefully selected parts of the application experiment to a different environment, a museum. For dissemination and transferability the experiment also established a small special interest group, whose members included cultural and educational organisations and multimedia technology professionals. Among the participants? future plans are to extend the experiment to other phases of the life-cycle and to use the results and experience gained from the experiment to other projects in their organisations, aiming at continuously improving the software process.

This report describes the most significant results of the experiment, experience gained and important lessons learned, concluding that software process improvement should be a continuous goal in the organisations, and continuous evaluation and commitment to quality by all people involved in the development should be the main ways to achieve these goals. The report also presents some problems encountered, especially when measuring the results of the experiment. It therefore interests multimedia applications developers and multimedia project managers, providing them with experiences, good and bad, gained from introducing best practices in multimedia applications development. This report may also interest organisations or individuals involved with education and culture, since they will discover the benefits of using multimedia technology as a means for distributing knowledge. Finally, anyone with a special concern for best software engineering practices, either as a software engineer or project manager, will be interested in the report since it presents experiences gained from an experiment which tries to adapt and apply state-of-the-art methodologies and tools in the area of educational multimedia applications development.

This report relates to work carried out by First Informatics SA, Lambrakis Research Foundation and Benaki Museum, in the framework of the ESSI Programme, with a financial contribution by the European Commission.

## 10.21   FLOWERPOWER 21677

### Process Improvement by Change of Paradigm in an Agriculture Company

The following report documents the way of Irsslinger company through the ESSI-21677 project with its work performed and the experiences gained.

The main target was to introduce the object oriented methodologies to restructure and improve the current (procedural) software engineering process. Through this change of paradigm it was expected, that new processes around software development would be introduced and existing processes would be improved. Further aims were to enhance communication with the SW users and to achieve a seamless transition from requirement specification through analysis to design and implementation. The improvement of effectiveness of the development process should lead to a higher quality of the final product in terms of robustness, stability, reliability and maintainability.

The experiences and the results of this experiment can be transferred to all SME´s with an own SW department who consider the introduction of object oriented techniques in their development process.

Due to the perception that better software products will have positive impact to the business at all, the results are of interest not only for software developers as well as to managers of such organisations.

To realise the above mentioned objectives a project team of 3 developers had to pass several phases of an exactly defined and scheduled workplan. The first phase of the experiment was training in basics of object oriented programming and development tools. This phase was followed by an so called "phase of individual reviewing", where the team could stabilise their knowledge in solving sample problems on their own. These exercises were necessary to start with the third and main phase, the re-engineering/redesign of the purchasing module of the Irsslinger application. The first steps in this phase led to a misconception in such a manner that the generated data model focused only the purchasing module and did not reflect the relations to the complete data base of Irsslinger. This mistake was corrected in starting a second time.

Another faced problem was the demand of the management, that the DataBase should be compatible with the existing, which required more time to realise than planned. These above mentioned reasons forced us to request the Commission for extending the project duration by 3 months.

After acceptance of prolongation the next steps were, on the basis of an extended data base model , to finish and stabilise the basic classes, to complete the application structure, to develop detail functions and procedures, to execute functional tests, to test user acceptance and evaluate the measured information during all phases.

Despite or because of the above difficulties we gained experiences from the FLOWERPOWER project in several areas. Not only the basis of OO SW development techniques but although a development tool-set existing of a workbench, a class library and a Data Dictionary.

The experiment showed us that strategies do exist, that secure a smooth transition from traditional practices to OO methodologies and that the adoption of OO techniques can bring significant benefits (after a long learning curve) as long as it is led by business needs and the top management supports this "technical change of paradigm" which is in all facets just so a "cultural change".

One of these benefits is the capability to realistic calculate the efforts and costs of program changes and extensions. The Irsslinger company will proof this in projects right after the experiment. Step by step the Irsslinger base line application will be transferred to object oriented structure.


# 10.22  ICONMAN 21379

## Implementing configuration management in very small enterprises

This report is based on work performed in the ICONMAN project during the 18 months (June 1996 - December 1997) of the process improvement experiment. The experiment was sponsored by the CEC under the ESSI Programme, project no. 21379.

The project's main goal was to implement configuration management in three small software companies and assess the effect of this effort.

The main conclusion from the project is: Implementing configuration management is worthwhile in very small companies. This is based on both qualitative and quantitative measurements and observations.

The companies have with respect to their own judgement successfully implemented routines for configuration management. Even though the process has been more demanding than expected, the maturing of the system development process was a necessary step in developing the business processes in the companies as a whole.

The main lessons learned were:

- Configuration management is a complex activity with far reaching consequences for the business as a whole.
- Implementing configuration management is an iterative process, and requires continuous refinement.
- In very small companies the introduction of configuration management should be tested in a controlled, but real-life environment.
- It was difficult to identify quantitative data to measure process performance, but the defined simple metrics were essential for evaluation of the experiment.
- The existence of an operative configuration management system has shown to make a positive impact on customer relations.
- The existence of an operative change request database has proven to be valuable in planning product releases.
- The existence of an operative configuration item library has proven to simplify the process of reconstructing earlier releases, and led to a higher service level for the customer.

## 10.23   IDIOM 10312

### Iterative Development Implementation of an Object-Oriented

The goal of the IDIOM project was to design a software development methodology which would help small organisations to improve their ability to develop, manage and maintain software. The methodology has the following characteristics;

- Suitable for small software development houses (typically < 20 software developers) operating in a real-time software environment.
- Based on object-oriented technology to maximise software reuse and increase return on investment.

The methodology was developed within a real software development environment; C-C-C Technology Limited (Northern Ireland). Although it is mainly of use to small software houses working within an object-oriented environment, anyone with an interest in process improvement or object-oriented technology may find parts of it relevant.

The key lessons learned were;

- The importance of having a defined methodology which covers the entire software lifecycle and the use of standard tools and techniques.
- The value of software process improvement in general.
- The relevance of the Bootstrap approach [Koch 1993] and the SEI Capability Maturity Model.
- The role of management in starting and maintaining process improvement efforts.
- An appreciation of the large investment in time and money which is required to support process improvement.
- The value of ESSI in helping small organisations to benefit from process improvement.

Using the methodology helped C-C-C technology to move from level 1 on the CMM scale to level 2 within the course of a year.

## 10.24  IMPACT 21628

### Improving Horizontal Activities In Project Execution Project Management, Configuration Management and Change Management

The main (i.e., experimental) part of the experiment was finished by the end of December 1996. Remaining workpackages essentially comprise termination, reporting and dissemination activities.

The process improvement experiment (PIE) provided us with an opportunity to experiment with and evaluate new methods, procedures and tools in a real life environment. To date the approach used proved itself to be extremely valuable.

By the experiment we aimed at sophisticated method and tool support to keep projects in line wrt effort, time and costs. Experience data collected in the project will be used for improved estimation and planning of future projects. Another objective was reliable and consistent managing of software documents and products of different versions. Furthermore, we aimed at reliable and fast handling of change requests. Finally, the motivation and skill of our employees to apply and continuously improve our quality management system should be developed.

In order to achieve these goals we established a project management method which is supported by the tools Microsoft Project and Excel. Furthermore, a configuration management system relying on the tool PVCS was applied to control the access to, and delivery of, all individual software documents belonging to a software product. Finally, a change management system was established for controlling and reporting change requests. This task is supported by the tool Change-Flow.

From a technological point of view we learned that an appropriate and comprehensive project plan, with estimated project parameter values (effort, time, costs) and continuously collected actual values from all professionals involved in the project, is crucial for successful project management. Though it is necessary to apply tools, we had to notice that Microsoft Project 4.0 doesn't serve for sufficient and adequate support in project management. As a kind of work-around we used a combination of Project and Excel for this purpose.

From a business point of view it became obvious that transparency of the software development process towards the own company management and to the business client, by delivering project management documents and periodical status reports, significantly improves confidence of all parties in the software process and the resulting products. Nevertheless, the application of tools is not for free and thus it is crucial for the success of changing established ways of working that the people concerned are convinced that the additional work eventually imposed on them will be for their own benefit.

The results of our experiment are of main interest to software suppliers and consultants in the area of technical and business orientated systems.

## 10.25  IMPOSE 23780

### Improving Object Oriented Methods in a Very Small Enterprise

This document is the Final report for the ESSI PIE project no. 23780; IMPOSE (Improving object oriented methods in a very small enterprise). IMPOSE has been executed by Invenia AS, a small Norwegian company (14 employees) producing tailor-made software (client/server) for customers, often on a fixed-price basis. In IMPOSE we aimed at enhancing our ability to make appropriate requirement specifications and time and cost estimates in order to gain better control with profit and use of resources, and to increase our ability to live up to customers expectations.

We have defined an object-oriented iterative software process model with four phases (envisioning, planning, developing, stabilising), based on the Microsoft Solution Framework, adjusted and detailed according to our needs. We are now using use cases (and prototypes) in order to elicit functional requirements, and follow the Unified Modelling Language for object-oriented analysis and design. Estimation is done in two stages, both during envisioning, and more precisely during planning. During the project we also evaluated and selected an object-oriented modelling tool, a document automation tool, and a requirements management tool, which now support the software process. The improved software development process with supporting tools has been used in two baseline projects.

In the first baseline project we are confident that the improved process helped us avoid irresponsible commitment and significant financial losses when we would not lower the fixed price in negotiations with the customer. With delivery on time and a total cost overrun of 20.7% for the second baseline project, it was within objectives defined (30% reduction in total overrun time and 20% reduction of financial losses). Both the management and developers of Invenia AS are generally very satisfied with the result of IMPOSE. We have decided to standardise on the new software process, which will be used in all new projects. It is also an important foundation for further improvements. In the near future we will focus on small-step improvements.

As an ESSI (European Systems and Software initiative) PIE (process improvement experiment), IMPOSE is funded by the Commission of the European Community.

## 10.26  IMPROVE-CM 21433

### Implementation of a Central Repository to Support Effective Configuration Management

This PIE experimented the effectiveness of the CM practices implemented using the Change Configuration Control (CCC)/ Harvest tool application [Ref. 1], to reduce the effort for S/W library management and to encourage the reusability of software modules for the Space Software Italia (SSI) projects. As expected, the enhancement mainly resulted in the improvement of the Change Control process for software and documentation that, thanks to this PIE, can now be made uniform and systematic for all projects. Furthermore, the analyses of achievements on the baseline project, encourage us to anticipate a major competitiveness due to costs reduction, with regard to Configuration Management activities, and an increased productivity in developing and maintaining software.

The baseline project for this PIE was the Assembly, Integration & Verification – Data Base Software (AIV-DB S/W) development project [Ref. 2]. It revealed to be a suitable pilot project for the purpose of this PIE: (1) its development schedule has satisfactorily overlapped the PIE timeframe; (2) its management plan was based on the parallel management of two different software versions (Maintenance of Release 1 and Development of Release 2), so demanding a more complex approach to Configuration Management.

AIV-DB is a database software product based on Oracle DB Management System; it is a flexible tool to control and manage the AIV activities during the development of systems of different size and complexity, such as Satellite, an high speed Train, or a Navy.

According to the PIE work plan and the proposed schedule, the following have been the main achievements:

- training activities have been performed on Assessment and Improvement methods and on the use of CCC/Harvest;

- a formal qualification of the PIE, in terms of an assessment of the SSI CM process, has been satisfactorily achieved and an improvement plan, identifying measures and indicators to monitor the PIE, has been finalised;
- a Software Life Cycle model, adequate for change control purposes, has been defined and set-up using CCC/Harvest, and its experimentation has been satisfactorily completed on the baseline project;
- a Software Problem Management model, fully integrated with the Software Life Cycle model, has been defined and set-up using CCC/Harvest, and its experimentation has been satisfactorily completed on the baseline project;
- metrics have been collected on the baseline project and their analysis has been performed for monitoring the actual CM process and provide corrective actions and evaluating the process improvement achievements;
- a Documentation life-cycle model, fully integrated with the Software Life Cycle model, has been defined and set-up using CCC/Harvest, and its experimentation has been satisfactorily completed on the baseline project;
- a common S/W repository, easily accessible from any SSI computer platform on the LAN, and even from authorised WAN nodes, has been established that will let all SSI employees to safely access and modify any S/W versions, without regard on which platform and where it was originally developed. We believe that this is a prerequisite for an easy and effective software reuse management and to increase productivity;
- a final evaluation of the experiment has been performed with a formal assessment of the resulting status of the PIE.

The use of a CM tool implementing advanced concepts (i.e., process modelling, parallel development) and a new approach (i.e., CCC/Harvest provides a unified framework supporting all the core functions in software development) has revealed beneficial for the baseline project, even if it has led to devote a particular effort in training people.

## 10.27   INCOME 21733

### Increasing Capability Level with Opportune Metrics and Tools

This final report illustrates the results of the ESSI project n. 21733, a Process Improvement Experiment (PIE), named INCOME (INcreasing Capability level with Opportune MEtrics and tools). The Project started in January the 15th 1996 and had a duration of 21 months.

The goal of the experiment was to demonstrate how the use of an assessment method such as SPICE [1] and a goal-oriented measurement approach like *ami* [2] along with specific tools can help a medium to large critical and complex software development project improve its development process in its weakest areas and maintain ISO 9001 compliance.

Finsiel, Italy's largest IT services and consultancy group, was the prime user in this experiment and no associated partners were involved. Finsiel's customers include central and local government departments, leading banks and large industrial groups.

The baseline project was a CASE tools development project, to which a significant number of resources are assigned each year in different geographical sites, and in which several innovative technologies are used.

The PIE is now completed and can be considered successful from several points of view:

- the approach followed in the experiment is valid, the adoption of SPICE and *ami* has been effective and the two methods appear to be complementary;
- the improvement actions defined and executed in the areas of the Project Management, Testing and Configuration Management caused a progress in the baseline project development process as shown by the specific indicators and by the process assessment performed at the end of the PIE applying the SPICE prospective standard;
- both the approach and some of the solutions within the improvement actions can be generalised and reused in a more general context within Finsiel and the IT community; indeed, a new improvement plan is being defined within a different Business Unit in Finsiel.


## 10.28   INFOS 21613

### Integrating Forward and Reverse Engineering of Object-Oriented Software

The software improvement experiment INFOS was jointly executed by the two companies Adtranz (business: railway systems) and ABB Calor Emag Schaltanlagen (business: switch gear). It aimed at improving the object-oriented software process in a running development project.

INFOS is now completed. In its first half the outline of an object-oriented software process was defined, which was successfully applied in work packages of the baseline project. CASE tools to support the software engineers in forward and reverse engineering were evaluated. The selected tool was used for requirements analysis, as well as for reverse engineering and automated documentation. In the second half of INFOS, the process model was extended by practices for design and reverse engineering. They were also applied in work packages of the baseline project. An analysis of results and impact closed INFOS.

The new software engineering practices have been surprisingly well received by software engineers and management. Many of the practices had quickly spread over the baseline project. For instance, the management of the baseline project adopted the incremental development model, which is part of the new software process. They used it for re-planning the baseline project. As a result, they reduced considerably the risk of project failure. An impact analysis calculated a business benefit by this change of process model of about 8 Million ECU.

Also for implementing the process improvement measures, an incremental and iterative style was applied. This style, which goes in short cycles through the loop "define practices – apply them – feedback experience", has turned out very effective.

In addition to the business benefit mentioned above, improvements of software quality, and enhancements of individual and organisational skills could be measured. They are substantiated by quantitative data.

The software process improvement project reported here was funded as a so called *Process Improvement Experiment* (PIE) by the ESSI program of the European Community (ESSI stands for *European System and Software Initiative*).

## 10.29  INTRA 10882

### In-Process Tracking and Reviewing Approach

INTRA is a Process Improvement Experiment supported by the European Commission under the European Systems and Software Initiative (ESSI) programme for Software Best Practices dissemination.

INTRA means "IN-process Tracking and Review Approach". The goal of this ESSI Application Experiment is to gain the well-known Inspection technology from IBM based on a "defects removal process" and to implement it on applications. The objective is to improve the quality of our software products and to reduce the software development life cycle time.

Within THOMSON-CSF, Inspections are called "In-Process Reviews" (IPRs). This is intended to emphasise that IPRs process is performed all along the software development life cycle, and not only at the end of development phases. The IPRs process is implemented in such a way that it fits with the Peer Reviews, a Level 3 key process area of the Capability Maturity Model of the SEI.

## 10.30  INTRASUPPORT 24085

### Software Project Support on the Intranet

Within ICL Finland, over 800 people develop software and applications in 4 cities across the country. Customer projects typically vary from 100 to 3000 man-days in volume. Therefore, the ability to increase the effectiveness and productivity of the software development processes is of key importance for the future success of the company.

The emphasis of the IntraSupport PIE project is on how to enhance communication in and between projects as well as how to store and re-use best practices learned in different projects. The theoretical base of the project is knowledge management. In the project, an environment has been built for creating, capturing, storing, sharing, and applying tacit and explicit knowledge in the team and organisation level. It is said that technology is only 1/3 of the success of a knowledge management project. Other enablers are organisational culture, leadership, and measurement. In this experiment the focus is on building the technology foundation, which we believe is a prerequisite for knowledge management in large information technology organisation. The other enablers have also taken into account for the project to succeed.

In ICL Finland improvements within software engineering projects have been achieved by developing, implementing, and storing a set of process and methodology templates, and deploying them as a part of the project management methodology on the intranet. The software engineering and project management methodology and processes have been used over the intranet for over a year now and the experiences have been encouraging. The current work goes one step further by creating systems for sharing and storing knowledge and information in and between projects. The project information sharing is based on web sites contain e.g. project documents, experience data on required tasks, their schedules and work efforts. The information is easily accessible within the intranet environment when defining new similar projects.

The results of this experiment are estimated along timetable predictability, work effort predictability, productivity, and the ease of use. Measurements will also include SPICE evaluations, function point analysis, intranet questionnaires, and interviews. In this experiment a case study has been made in order to examine the effects of the intranet on project management and software engineering. Results of the experiment are guiding because most of the effects will be actualised in long term. However, through the experiment better visibility and easier communication will be achieved as well as increased capability and productivity.

## 10.31   IRIS 10509

### Improving Reuse in Space

This report presents the final results of the IRIS (Improving Reuse in Space) experiment, developed with support of the European Commission. Its main goal is to study potential improvements of the normal software life cycle used in space projects, addressed to increase software reusability in this field without handicapping other essential quality factors.

To achieve this goal, a subset of components from a typical space application has been selected and *developed FOR reuse*. Then the resulting components have been evaluated in terms of their quality and reusability potential, and finally a comparison study has also been made with respect to the use of a more traditional approach.

Key lessons learned during this experiment have been as follows:

- Tools can help, but they do not change processes by themselves. They are worthless (even unsuitable) when they are not introduced in parallel to the proper organisational changes.
- Potential reusability of a component is not easy to quantify. This is in part due to the relative immaturity of software measurement discipline.
- Generality and performance must be balanced in this domain. Performance penalties must be minimised. Duplication of critical sections due to generality must be avoided. In particular, low level components are not well-suited for re-use, due to their strong hardware dependency.
- Ada is not a panacea for software reusability. Some environments are very disappointing in the implementation of most advanced features, so you are forced to carefully employ them.

After this experiment, next step is to promote *development WITH reuse* within the company. In this way, return on investment will be obtained by reusing the developed components.

Results of this experiment should be specially relevant to those readers working in one or several of the following areas: development of onboard real-time embedded systems, use of CASE tools, small-scale reusable components, and software quality measurement.


## 10.32  ISORUS 10936

### Implementation and Evaluation of a Software Reuse Methodology

The ISORUS project aimed to develop and evaluate a methodology to introduce Reuse in the Software process at ELIOP. Its objectives were to reduce costs and time-to-market, and improve software reliability, by means of the introduction of systematic reuse practises. The project was undertaken by ELIOP as the single contractor, with some support from external subcontractors.

ELIOP SA is a Spanish company with 100 employees, 30 of them directly involved in SW engineering. Its main activity is the delivery of Industrial Control Systems, including software for standard computers and embedded into microprocessor-based in-house manufactured equipment. Such systems require real time, continuous operation, and often they are controlling critical industrial processes. Software is a very important part of the added value of ELIOP products.

The work performed started with the identification of an adequate reuse approach, a review of the current practises and definition of the specific improvements to be made. After that, appropriate metrics were identified, needed tools were selected and installed, and required training activities were done. The experimentation itself included the identification, development and use of the reusable assets. Final stages of the project included a review of the procedures and an evaluation of the results of the experiment and the human and organisational aspects of software reuse practises. As a result, a planning for introduction of the improvements as a regular practise in ELIOP was done.

Key lessons learned from the project are the following ones:

- Reuse of other assets apart from code is very important.
- Introduce Domain analysis to allow a systematic reuse of software within a specific domain of application.
- It is necessary to have strong configuration management practises in place for all software assets in order to carry out reuse successfully.
- To reduce risks, allow to modify the software assets when reused, if necessary. This decreases costs and has lower organisational impact.
- An appropriate level of process and product Quality is a prerequisite to introduce Reuse. Productivity benefits will appear only after introducing the necessary quality improvements.
- Consider human and organisational barriers when introducing reuse. To overcome them, define explicitly your process and all organisational roles, and keep managers and developers informed as closely as possible.
- In order to facilitate reuse, the organisation must define a business strategy looking beyond the current projects, anticipate needs and define product lines.
- To reduce risks, do improvements based on an evolutionary, step-by-step approach, rather than a "revolutionary" approach.

As a result of the experiment, ELIOP is introducing the experienced methodology as a regular practise.

## 10.33  ISOTOPO 21603

### Integrated Software Management Through Process Improvement

The objective of the Process Improvement Experiment (PIE) ISOTOPO was to improve the competitive position of IBERMATICA in its market. Prior to the experiment it was established, by the strategic analysis performed in the ongoing long term project MIDAS, the key factor need to improve the competitive position, in short: better service, in providing improved products to the customers, and professionalism with fulfilment of commitments.

Guided by the strategic plan, the experiment starts with a focused assessment of the software process in the areas related to the factors which control the competitive position. Following the assessment results, three parallel working groups were set up assigned to the three selected improvement areas:

- Requirement Management
- Software Project Planning, and projects tracking and oversight.
- Software Testing

Previously a model was selected to guide the assessment and the improvement, the model selected was the SEI's CMM.

In order to obtain these objectives a number of preparative actions oriented to assure the success of the experiment were also carried out:

- Training and promotion in the necessary techniques and methods in order to go ahead the improvement process; including training in effective team work.
- Assess the Area situation of the software production processes, against the selected reference model: CMM.
- Define the Unity strong and weak points and identify the priority improvement key areas.
- Investigate the state of the art in Software Integrated Process management.

The improved process definition has been carried out by the Working groups in participative and collaborative fashion, that is one of the key success factors. Work performed included:

- Carry out the improvement actions that meet the Area necessities, regarding mainly the client attention and the productivity improvement.
- Define the procedures that solve the key area of Requirements Management and Preparation for testing in pilot projects.
- Define the procedures for the Planning and tracking Area and oversight and tracking projects.
- Define the software procedure and testing techniques.
- Test the defined procedures in pilot projects.
- Procedures Optimising.
- To continue with the Procedures Institutionalisation Plan in the whole Organisation.

The analysis of the final results show that the main points of the objectives were reached and the effect in face of the customers involved in the pilots phase has been positive with a high level of satisfaction and excellent evaluations of the qualification and professionalism of the staff and of the process defined.

As a conclusion we can state that our process improvement experiment was successfully.

## 10.34  LANHOBEK 24155

### Client Relationships and Requirements Management Improvement

The objective of the experiment was to establish and institutionalise management and engineering practices in the area of Acquisition, Definition and Management of User Requirements, in order to proceed with more stable specification downwards.

A working group within the internal structure was created, with user participation and the assistance of an external consultancy company, with a primary focus on technology transfer to the organisation. Quality assurance activities and processes were defined in this experiment to the extent of the Requirement processes, including acceptance tests. Other QA activities will be established in the future.

New processes for Requirement Management and Requirement Definition were developed, tested and managed in the organisation within a pilot project.

Some project objectives (increase in customer satisfaction, reduction of development time and maintenance costs) were nearly reached with significant advances and other (reduction of time-to-market, increase in software production, rise a level in SPICE processes related to requirements) were widely surpassed. The new processes are clearly useful in the organisation, helping to improve the service to the clients.

The organisation is working to institutionalise the new processes, following a plan that was developed in the last phase of the project.

This Process Improvement Experiment (PIE), named as LANHOBEK, was run by Lantik, S.A. as prime user without associated partners, and has been 100% funded by the European Commission, DG III, within the European Systems & Software Initiative (ESSI) in the Information Technologies programme (ESPRIT).

## 10.35  LARGECM 21473

### Configuration Management in the LARGE

The LARGECM experiment is related to research carried out by Alenia in the frame-work of the ESSI Community Program with financial contribution by the Commission.

The experiment concerns the improvement of the Configuration Management practice by moving from traditional version control of sources (SCCS like) to a comprehensive Configuration Management System.

The new Software Configuration Management activity cover all process artefacts, on a large and varied set of hardware/software platforms, assuring data integrity, inter-operability, improving security and automating main configuration management practices.

The Alenia's Needs for an advanced Configuration Management have been identified doing interviews to a selected pool of specialists and managers; the needs have been deduced from the perceived Configuration Management limitations.

Analysis of CM available Commercial tools has been done to identify the right tool to use for the needs of the Alenia Radar System Division; that is reported in the document provides "CM Technology Selection".

A CM Product Model has been defined as a collection of linked artefacts (resulting from the software development/maintenance process).

The main CM practices (Process Model) have been formalised, rigorously modelled and their enactment (execution) have to be supported by a process/workflow engine.

Integration and consistency of the Process Model and the Product Model has been of primary concern. Conformance with ISO CM requirements (i.e. ISO 9004-7) has been the target.

The experiment has had the purpose to identify the software configuration items and to carry out a systematic control of its changes, in order to maintain its integrity and traceability throughout all Life Cycle phases.

The new software CM system has been implemented by Alenia/DSR Software Unit, with the selected Technology, and then used on the baseline project evaluating the benefits.

The baseline project has been the Reply Processor & Channel Management (RPCM) and the Operator Control Panel (OCP) Computer Software Configuration Items (CSCIs) of the SIR-S secondary radar.

The management organisation and resources applied to this baseline project, procedures, methods, tools and facilities to implement Configuration Management activities during the software life cycle have been described in the Software Configuration Management Plan.

Benefits for involved people result in enhancement the efficiency of the software maintenance and its reuse. These aspects all contribute to increase the overall competitiveness on the market.

This experiment contribute at on going standardisation efforts, CM practice is intended to be institutionalised as part of company Quality System.

## 10.36  MARITA 10549

### Management of a Flexible and Distributed Software Production

This paper deals with the experience ABB Robotics Products AB have gained during the transition from a traditional functional project development to a continuous component-oriented process, i.e. to build products from components, a process which an increasing number of companies may be forced to adopt to remain competitive. This implies using object-oriented technologies to promote reuse.

The aim of a component-based development process is to shorten lead times to market, enabling developers to "snap together" generic components and customise them for local market requirements, or specific market segments, as these arise. Cycle time is shortened if "component development" and "product assembly" is done in parallel and if customisation can take place locally, implying the need for distributed support for component-oriented development.

The ESSI experiment, MARITA, had the goal to identify the configuration management processes needed to support component-oriented development and to automate as many of these processes as possible through the use of tools. It was found more difficult than anticipated to adopt existing tools on the market to the component-oriented process. During the experiment a number of project organisational changes had to be added. Even the development model had to be redefined. ROP does not claim the measures taken are the only possible or the best ways, there are still things to improve, but it has improved the maturity of ROP as a software supplier.

The MARITA experiment have been carried out within the framework of the ESSI Community Research Programme with a financial contribution by the Commission.

## 10.37   MASLYD 24287

### Metrics & Software Lifecycle Definition

ICE Computer Services identified the need for significant process improvement in various aspects of it's Software Department's activities as a result of a TRI-SPIN project in March 1996. The Software Department's primary activity is development and support of a Software Product for the Financial sector, also does an amount of bespoke software development. The findings identified a number of major shortcomings in the operations of this department which are typical of many small Software Development organisations, namely : Over dependence on specific staff for Product Knowledge in the department, unreliability of the Cost Estimation processes in place. Difficulty for new hires due to lack of clearly documented procedures and work practices. This PIE was initiated with the intention of addressing these issues.

The major lessons we have learned are (1) the potential for improvement was greater than originally envisaged and (2) the process of reviewing specific problems forced us to reconsider and confirm precisely what the business of the department is.

We have already achieved significant benefits from this process and believe that we have established a basis for further improvements as the processes developed and implemented are further refined with use. The knowledge gained from this activity should be of interest to many other small Software Development organisations many of whom have very similar problems as identified in ICE.

## 10.38   MAUSE 10560

## A Methodological Approach in the Use of Software Engineering

This paper describes the results of the MAUSE (ESSI-10560) project. This project was a Process Improvement Experiment (PIE) supported by the early phase of the ESSI programme. MAUSE was carried out by two Small to Medium Enterprises (SMEs) which aimed at assessing the benefits of adopting a methodical approach to S/W development. The approach taken was to adopt a methodology framework for analysis-design and project management assisted by design and development tools. MAUSE was based on the integration of the following components:

- A formal requirements and analysis and design process (SSADM).
- A solid management framework (PRINCE).
- CASE support to improve the productivity of the Analysis and Design (Systems Architect).
- GUPTA development environment to support windows user interface development including prototyping to provide portability, scalability and operation in Client-Server mode.
- The measurement basis of the experiment was set up according to DESMET (a methodology for determining an appropriate evaluation method for new methods/tools, funded by UK Dept. of Trade & Industry), and MERMAID E-2046 for software cost estimation.

Although the metrics taken do not show dramatic improvements in productivity the overall quality of the software has significant raised. The main benefits in MAUSE which are the dramatic improvement of maintainability of software and product quality, come from the adoption of the methodological framework. In addition, the SSADM framework encouraged a formal and professional interaction with the clients. The use of CASE within this project was mainly to facilitate documentation. The adoption of the development platform has given a number of benefits mainly in the area of prototyping. Observable improvements were taken in the following areas:

- The SSADM methodology ensured that requirements, design and implementation documentation was produced in a standard, generally accepted format, therefore, the communication between the software development team members has been enhanced.

- The availability of prototypes allowed the customer early visibility of the "look-feel" of the product and, again, led to the identification of defects prior to implementation.
- For the products developed in MAUSE, no support has been required and no defects reported in the first 3 months after their release.
- Reuse of screens/forms was enabled.
- The amount of code produced was substantially decreased.
- The data collected during the experiment has provided an effort estimation model that can be used to assist the costing of future products.

This experiment should be of interest to Small companies producing bespoke or packaged commercial data processing software, who currently use informal software production methods. Both companies participating in the experiment regard the project approach as proven and are adopting it throughout their organisations.

## 10.39  MAZPIE 21411

### Software Development Process Improvement Experiment

This report describes the results of ESSI Project No 21411, MAZ PIE. The project has been completed after two extensions in time at the end of November 1997. The work done in this project has been supported by the European Commission. The Commission owns the copyright of this report. The report is public and may be disseminated freely.

The project is concerned with the introduction of methods and tools to improve software development with respect to object-oriented analysis & design (OOA/OOD) as well as configuration management (CM).

This report is primarily written for software developers and software development managers. It is consequently addressing software houses as well as all companies with at-least a medium-sized software development department (e.g. 5-15 employees).

This PIE has been submitted as a direct consequence of a formal BOOTSTRAP assessment, which ranked the software processing unit involved at 1.25, among other reasons due to the lack of a formal quality system, replicable software design processes, and configuration management. A quality system in accordance with ISO-9001 has meanwhile been installed through efforts outside this PIE.

The PIE is designed to address some of the remaining shortcomings. In the course of the experiment appropriate tools have been selected and are subsequently applied to a baseline project. The PIE includes training on methods and tools for the staff involved. The PIE has three primary goals:

- Improvement of software development by object-oriented analysis & design and configuration management
- Incorporation of these methods and tools into the quality management system in which the software engineering sub-model of the V-Model has been adapted to the organisation's needs to describe the software process. This must be extended to include regulations for object-orientation and reuse.

and in the consequence

- Increase of BOOTSTRAP ranking to 2.5-3.0.

Here are some of the more general key lessons:

- Acceptance in the company is high because management is dedicated to quality improvement and developers are young (usually graduates from university) and eager to learn new things.
- Selection of appropriate tools is a complex task that must not be underestimated. In order to minimise efforts use evaluation reports, experience reports, and strong filter criteria to reduce the number of tools to look at.
- Even if properly selected, introduction and application of new tools and methods will not be smooth and much time will be spent to cope with unanticipated difficulties.
- With OOA/OOD, consistency between analysis, design, and implementation is high for the static architecture of a program, it is however not supported for its dynamic architecture.
- With CM, build times for release builds have been reduced by up to 80%.

A final BOOTSTRAP assessment resulted in a ranking of 2.25 for the entire software processing unit, and 2.5 for the PIE's base-line project. Aspects related most closely to the PIE objectives where rated at up to 3.0.

## 10.40   MBM 21476

### Management by Metrics

Management by Metrics "MBM" experiment concerns metrics collection and exploitation in support of managers to gain an improvement in the software process.

Alenia and Intecs Sistemi have already in place a defined process including the collection of many process and product metrics. However these metrics are often just thrown into a database for statistical purposes. Rarely they have a direct impact on the same process they are taken from. MBM intends to bring back those metrics into the process, for the benefit of the process.

The MBM experiment has the goal to provide a Software process and product indicators "Metrics" with a friendly user presentation. The indicators are depending on the company goals. Practised deployment of Management by Metrics is expected to move from actual level 3 (of both Intecs and Alenia) to perform a project working at maturity level 4.

Inside the experiment execution, firstly technical and managerial aspects have been selected as related domain to be improved ("Company Business Goals" selection), then AMI method (Application of Metrics in Industry) rigorous approach has been applied and the detailed "metrication plan" has been derived. Automatic Support Tool(s) have been delivered and Metrics collection has started (and is currently running) to feed the "dashboard" in the two companies.

The metrics viewer "dashboard", is a highly intuitive, user-friendly presentation tool selected among commercial off-the-shelf (COTS) available solutions. The "dash-board" experimented on two quite different baseline projects, provide the managers (and quality managers), at a glance and graphically, all basic process indicators, including planned vs. actual vs. historical, flagging warning and alarm values. On a mouse click, basic process indicators show up into sub-dash-boards to provide more detailed indicators, up to the level of detail required. Management decisions (e.g. when to stop testing, increase the staff, postpone a release, improve inspections, trigger an audit on a subcontractor, etc.) are taken on a quantitative basis. Managers become familiar to read these dash-boards and to understand their dynamics. The "in action" phase for managers community has run: the benefits for involved people are therefore evident and valuable.

The Alenia and Intecs dash-board are not identical – because each company has its own business goals, Software Architecture and development Platforms. The Priorities are different and different indicators are necessary; nevertheless the "harmonisation" of the two dash-boards has been pursued with a benefit for the projects. Partnership between Alenia and Intecs Sistemi optimises the overall experiment effort and makes a first generality attempt for the great potential of technology transfer to other organisations. Differences between the two MBM-experiment "implementation details" are identified in the rest of the document.

At the conclusion of the experiment the result of SPICE assessment can be summarised as follows:

- for Alenia although the selected processes have not reached the capability level 4, their execution provides the opportunity to other process to be executed at level 4.
- for Intecs Sistemi: the capability level 4 has been reached.

This experiment is contributing at on going standardisation efforts, the Management by Metrics practice is intended to be institutionalised as part of both companies Quality Systems. The dash-board is near to become an integral appendix of all project progress reports.

MBM experiment is related to research carried out by Alenia as Prime and Intecs Sistemi as Associated Partner in the frame work of the ESSI Community Program with financial contribution by the Commission.

## 10.41   METPRO 21323

### Company Metrics Programme Introduction : A Quantitative Approach to Software Process Understanding and Improvement

The objective of the experiment has consisted in understanding the software engineering practice (and then software quality and productivity) by measurement of the product and process.

The goal was to start a company metrics programme in order to drive a software process understanding and improvement. The main goals of the metrics program were:

- to provide the quantitative information essential to identify opportunities for improvement;
- to verify the advantages of the implemented changes to the development process.

The experiment has consisted on understanding and quantifying the shortcomings relevant to the following areas:

- software problem analysis and defects prevention capability;
- productivity and schedule estimation capability.

The experience gained with the execution of the experiment is fully transferable to all the companies developing software which decide to better understand and improve their development process.

The primary area/community of interest to which the experiment corresponds is:

- Industrial sector: Information Technology (any system and software supply company)
- Community of interest – System point of view: Technically oriented systems
- Community of interest – Technology point of view: any software application using high level languages, software product technology and an established process method.

The work done regards the definition of the metric program plan, described in the Annex A, the data gathering for the baseline projects, their re-engineering in electronic sheets designed by us and data validation respect to the established metrics. The results are complete for all the baseline projects and they are reported in the Annex B.

The potential for replicating the results of the experiment is due to the fact that the proposed method and metrics framework present the following advantages:

- they are life cycle independent, so their use is not affected by various development methodologies which could be utilised;
- they are simple to understand and easy to apply.

## 10.42 MIDAS 21244

# Measurable Improvement of Development Deployment and Operation of Interbank Automation Software

The MIDAS project aims at a measurable improvement in the reliability and availability of interbank services offered by SIA, the organisation in charge of running, developing, and maintaining the National Interbank Network of Italy. Such improvement is achieved by establishing an effective CM process, i.e. to define CM procedures and policies, to select and customise automated tools supporting CM activities and to experiment the new CM process in a baseline project. A suitable measurement program was defined – using the Goal/Question/Metrics (GQM) technique – and executed in order to objectively assess the effectiveness of the new CM practice.

This document describes the achievements of the MIDAS project. The document is addressed to both managers and technical people. In fact both organisational and business-oriented issues, as well as technical information (mainly excerpts from the deliverables) are reported, in order to provide a picture of the project as comprehensive as possible, and to allow readers to be informed about all relevant issues concerning the establishment of CM and measurement processes.

### Work Done

CM policies and tools: this is the core activity of the project, since CM is the main innovation introduced in SIA with the experiment [1]. The following steps were performed:

Definition of the CM process for the pilot project development environment. The pilot project is the NRO project. NRO will provide a full range of services for the management and operation of the SIA network. It also provides APIs and interfaces to allow SIA customers to interface their own applications with SIA services.. It is one of the most strategic product that SIA will deliver in the next five years.

- Selection and customisation of a supporting tool (CCC/Harvest).
- Deployment of the CM system for the NRO software, training of NRO project people, establishment of an on-line support service (help desk).
- Optimisation of the CM system, according to the results of measurements, monitoring, problem reports and spontaneous feed-back.
- Definition of the GQM plan and the measurement plan to assess the effectiveness of introducing CM in SIA.
- Execution of the GQM measurement program: results are reported in [3,13] and briefly outlined in section 4.1 of this document
- External dissemination: the MIDAS project, its objectives and results have been presented in several conferences and meetings.

Internal dissemination: MIDAS objectives and technical and managerial implications were discussed in SIA, involving both people from the pilot project, people from other projects and departments, and also some suppliers.

Lessons learned in the project and reported in this document concern the establishment of CM in a controlled way (with a special reference to the integration of process modelling, improvement and measurement), optimisations of the process (specially as far as data collection, process monitoring, support and enforcing are concerned), tool selection and customisation, management and cost issues.

## 10.43   MMM 21718

### Metrics, Measurement and Management

KoDa GmbH, a small business software developing enterprise has conducted a process improvement experiment (PIE), that is financially supported by the EU within the ESSI programme.

This PIE was targeted to introduce measurement in the software engineering of the company.

The chosen approach was the Goal Question Metric method after the first preparatory steps of the PIE.

Following this methodical approach lead to the discovery of insufficient process descriptions, to the refinement of the process and the introduction of additional process steps.

This forced our focus on the guideline to keep things simple and the target to allow for measurement activities in the future not more than 4% of project effort.

The conclusion of the PIE is that measurement is possible even in a small company but care must be taken with the first difficult steps in order to control effort and cost. We had no difficulties with regard to personal objections but a lot of engagement of our engineers due to the open cultural climate of our company. But in the longer run we recognised that additional measures have to be taken to keep the motivation and attitude to support this PIE and the goals behind it.

The strategy to rely on good consulting in parallel with our own studies of literature and the approach to first try to manage our task by available means and organisation and then look for tool support was right for us but we were aware of the high costs of doing so and now we desire to have simple tools for our needs available at the market.

Measurement is not only possible in a SME but also worthwhile. The investment can be controlled and the value can directly be related to the goals. There are also – in our case at least (see annex 9.7) – unintended advantages if you promote and maintain a measurement culture, keep an open mind, allow for flexibility and support responsibilities and competence of your project leaders and engineers.

Available within our company is now an environment for effort collection and the various GQM and measurement plans according to GQM as well as a history database to store the main results and support estimations.

## 10.44  MOODISC 21416

### Methods for Object Oriented Design and Implementation Supporting Changes

The implementation of this project and the results of this project are of interest for SMEs with development and maintenance of large and complex software systems, which want to improve their configuration and change management and/or their development processes.

The companies Micrologica GmbH and Phoenix Contact GmbH & Co have worked together in this project to improve their software processes and to gain experiences for other companies in similar situations. Both companies have since some years quality management systems, which are certified according to ISO 9001, but they have been awaked further to improve their processes. Each partner has had experiences on the field that was of interest for the other and could exchange it to the other partner. Between both partners there is no competition in business fields.

Micrologica's objectives have been to improve the Configuration and Change Management (CCM) for development, customising and maintenance of its software products in order to save time in these process phases and to consolidate the base for a stable quality. Phoenix Contact's objectives have been to introduce Object Oriented Analysis and Design methods (OOA/OOD), to improve the reusability of software elements by this means and to shorten the time to market for its products.

To detect the gained benefits the basic idea of this PIE has been: Assessments of the SW-processes before and after all improvements in both companies will show the improvements of the processes. At the beginning of the PIE assessments of SW-processes have been carried out in both companies to get Bootstrap like process-profiles as a base for the comparison after the PIE. These profiles have shown that Micrologica has been rather weak in CCM-methods and -tools and that Phoenix Contact has been rather weak in the methodology for analysis and design.

In the preparation phase of the project all members of the involved staff have been trained for the usage of suitable CCM-methods and -tools respectively for proven OOA/OOD-methods. In the experimental phase these techniques have been established and used in the baseline projects of both companies successfully.

Micrologica has worked out detailed user guides and special labour instructions for handling of projects and files for different groups of development problems, customisation and maintenance. The selected CCM-Tool is suitable very well for development problems with a great number of files and a high rate of multi-used files in different projects. It has enough flexibility for customisation and maintenance processes also. In this way the developments under CCM save time and have higher reliability. Measurements during the PIE have delivered characteristic dates of all CCM-actions:

To hold older versions and configurations with their history in an efficient way gives more flexibility and also more safety for development, customisation and maintenance of large software systems.

About a third of all modules are reused now by sharing from other projects. This gives a high reliability and saves development time and costs.

Although the number of installed systems for customers has quadruplicated throughout the PIE and despite a new software version was introduced at the last one third of the PIE, the number of all errors found in these systems has only triplicated in this time. The average error rate at the end of the PIE is about one error per installed system per quarter of a year and is decreasing more rapidly.

The effort for debugging of the errors of all installed systems decreases about 25 per cent in a quarter.

For Micrologica the assessments after the PIE have shown, that the total score for all attributes of the Configuration and Change Management has been doubled against that at the start of the PIE.

Phoenix Contact has chosen and adopted the OO methodology, which was used for some years at Micrologica and which was developed by the STC (Software Technique Centre of the University of Hamburg) originally for banking applications.

User guide lines and labour instructions for the OOA/OOD methods have been worked out and this OOA/OOD-methods were applied for the development of new functions in the baseline project of Phoenix Contact. To support the OO methods furthermore a new evolutionary development life cycle model was explored in this experiment which supports the OO methods much better than the traditional waterfall model used before this experiment.

The chosen OO methods could be applied successful. The development in the experimental phase was performed without tool support to get used to the new methods. We found that manually maintenance of development documents is rather cumbersome without tool support. Therefore we've checked whether a CASE tool could be applied for design and maintenance and found out, that this is possible and that this reduces the effort for complex designs.

This PIE has increased the skill of the developers and the awareness of the importance of software process in general and especially of usefulness of measurements. There are clear indications, that the improved software architecture reduces development time for changes and additions, but this could not be proven within this experiment because there was no redesign phase.

The process improvement gained by the experiment at Phoenix Contact was measured by assessments after the PIE. The total score for requirements engineering, design and implementation has been doubled against that at the start of the PIE.

This project has been carried out in the Specific RTD Programme of ESSI and was supported financially by the European Commission. The partners wish to acknowledge the European Commission for their subsidy and also for their organisational assistance to accomplish this project.

# 10.45  MSI-QBP 21547

## Maritime Safety Information using Quality Best Practice

By means of this PIE Gepin Engineering Spa aimed to set up a centralised Software Quality Management (SQM) function with the role of driving and assuring the quality of both software processes and products developed and maintained in the company. The present PIE represented a substantial step towards such a goal, focusing, in particular, the improvement effort on the most critical supporting processes (for the company), that are Configuration and Change Management (CCM) and Documentation Development Management (DDM). The PIE was managed on top of a baseline project, relevant for the company, concerned with the treatment of Maritime Safety Information. The topics of the baseline project together with the subject of the software Quality Best Practices gave the title to the PIE.

### The Results Concern

- well experimented and wide company accepted procedures and templates for managing Documentation Development and System Configuration/Change processes
- customised support tools for the PIE focused processes: Lotus Notes for the Documentation Development Management process; CCC/Harvest for the Configuration and Change Management process
- well experimented and wide company accepted Software Process Improvement (SPI) and measurement schemes, managed respectively by the SPICE and the AMI frameworks.

### Key Lessons Learned

- About SPI
- SPI strictly depends on top management commitment and involvement
- SPICE and AMI can be complementary frameworks for SPI strategies
- About DDM and CCM processes

They positively influences improvement of both SLC Engineering and management processes because are the basis for:

- SLC documents produced according to well-established workflow models, to well defined documentation requirements, to well experimented documentation templates
- SLC workproducts under configuration and change control during the whole project lifetime
- effective project measurement and control
- About the selected technologies (Lotus Notes and CCC/Harvest)
- The Notes application (customisation of Lotus Notes environment) currently:
- drives every user to follow the planned document life cycle
- tracks all steps in the document life cycle
- allows full-text search in documents, improving document usability and reuse
- allows easy verification of planned life cycle compliance In the future, the Notes application will also allow:
- to get statistics on document management process
- to verify the project documents' progress
- CCC/Harvest is:
- a distributed environment for configuration management, accessible to all team people
- an environment easy to learn and to use

In the future CCC/Harvest environment will be more flexible and will allow an easy tailoring to suit the configuration management environment to several project needs.

### Relevance and Applicability of the Results to the Wider Community

The potential users interested in the results of the MSI_QBP experiment are the many European SMEs working in Information Technology, because of the worry of competition and quality costs. The reference to well recognised international software engineering and quality standards, in the implementation of the SQM procedural and template framework, as well as the adoption of commercially available support tools allow the project results to constitute a well founded and repeatable framework for European software SMEs that would start an SQM program.

Also the approach followed by Gepin could be of interest of the wider community. It was based on the assumption that the improvement on a software process does not depend on the sophistication degree of technology. This one provides technicalities to manage base practices of a process, but does not provide features to institutionalise a process in a company. This require a well recognised improvement scheme which offers the way to reach a step by step process management capability spreading on the range of the process planning, measurement & tracking, documentation, standardisation, etc. practices.

## 10.46   ODAGUI 10995

## Open Database and GUI Framework

This application experiment, Open Database and GUI Framework (ODAGUI), concentrates on introducing object-oriented methods and tools which make possible to develop a new generation of GUI and relational database applications based on existing systems. Together with the promises of possible reusability and quality improvements independency of database vendors is sought with new techniques and tools.

The tools chosen (Visual C++$^{TM}$, odb++ and SQL-Retriever$^{TM}$) have proven that they can deliver the objectives of the application experiment. An OPAC application with a graphical user interface and database independent structure has been tested with several databases.

However, for the business release version of the OPAC application we chose a different approach. To limit the clients required resources to a minimum we transferred the database operations to a process located on the server. The communication between the client and server processes is directed through an interpreter process located at the client.

Transition to a totally new approach in software engineering can't be achieved in a short period. Demands for fast results can lead to inadequate designs that utilise object-oriented techniques only partially. Therefore, straight forward productivity and quality improvements need more training, investments and time.

This report could interest companies that are going to invest on object-oriented techniques or database independent programming in the Microsoft Windows environment.

## 10.47   PASS 21223

## Payroll Accounting and Settlement System

PASS (Payroll Accounting and Settlement System project is the first Central and Eastern European ESSI PIE project directly supported by the European Commission. The PASS project is carried out under the ESSI initiative with the financial support of the Commission of the European Communities under the ESPRIT Programme EP21223.

The PASS (Payroll Accounting and Settlement System) project started as a new business project of MemoLuX. Its business purpose is to develop a modular, platform independent, integrated networked software system satisfying functional requirements of EU standards in public accountancy and applicable for the Hungarian as well as for the international market. The system provides direct service among Employers, Employees and Banks. The PASS project is the baseline project for the Process Improvement Experiment.

In the PIE the quality of MemoLuX´s development process was enhanced to become well defined and predictable, and during the dissemination supported by ISCN this PIE is used as a master example to adapt Eastern European processes to the high quality norms of Western Europe, this way facilitating the integration of Eastern Europe into a joint EU in the long term.

Objectives and expected results are improving the control of the development process (QA Unit, structured system analysis, improved testing process, efficient project planning, ISO 9001 documentation), raising the maturity level (CMM) to 3 and achieving compliance with ISO 9001 requirements at this high level of maturity.

Relevant Industrial Sector: BC IS (Business, legal and management consultancy, holdings; Software consultancy and supply, Data processing and related services)

Community of Interest – Systems Point of View: Business Orientated Systems

Community of Interest – Technology Point of View:

Application Attributes: Life Cycle Management, Life Cycle Independent Functions

Product Technology: OOP, Quality Management

Process Method: BOOTSTRAP, Project planning, Structured System Planning Methodology

## 10.48  PCS 24065

## Project Management and Engineering Global Control System

This PIE (Process Improvement Experiment) was concerned with improving the software configuration management and version control systems used by Clockworks. The immediate objective and expected result was to reduce the incidence of configuration errors and the work involved in correcting these errors.

Part of the experiment involved looking for suitable software configuration management tools for use in localisation projects. However, our experience to date has been that there is no single tool that could be used to manage the thousands of separate items, the great number of versions, and the diversity of applications that a localisation project requires. Instead our solution uses a semi-automated system consisting of a Lotus Notes database, some file management tools (i.e. FileSync), a new directory structure, and naming convention and new procedures, and it relies on people to follow these procedures.

The localisation of "Oil Change", a product from Cybermedia Corporation, was selected to be the baseline project where the new procedures and technology were tested and metrics were collected. In the project very significant improvements in the configuration failure rate and repeat failure rate were experienced when the new system and procedures were introduced.

Due to the success of this experiment, Clockworks plans to use a generalised version of the new system and procedures in all its projects.

From the technological point of view the next stage is to publish the Notes data to the Web so that the customer and contractors that are involved in a localisation project have direct access to information about it. Also we plan to increase the functionality of the current Lotus Notes system.

The experience gained in this PIE is useful for many European localisation specialists, since they confront the same problems as Clockworks in managing their localisation work. Other localisation companies will be able to adopt similar approaches to those demonstrated in this PIE, and will have access to the same technical and commercial benefits.

The European Commission has supported this Process Improvement Experiment by contributing 270.790 ECU.

## 10.49  PERSPI 24158

### Personal Software Process Improvement

The purpose for the PERSPI project is to improve the way individuals perform their day-to-day software development activities. More specifically, PERSPI is an attempt to introduce the PSP methodology in an industrial environment, putting emphasis on its gradual employment in real-life projects, rather than on an introduction through formal and long-term training. The PERSPI project is a bottom-up approach, in contrast to the previous top-down process improvement efforts, for the improvement of the quality of the delivered products at the finest level of the development process, i.e. the individuals. The main objectives of introducing PSP in the development process is to increase quality (by reducing the Defects/Error rates), enhance predictability, increase job satisfaction and in the long term increase the productivity in a quantified and disciplined manner.

In the context of the PERSPI experiment the PSP has been thoroughly studied in order to design and formally introduce the CL_PSP1 and CL_PSPR1 processes (modified and customised PSP for the Computer Logic's production line) in the Coding and the Report development processes of the Omega S/W production environment. The results achieved by the introduction of PSP in the context of the PERSPI experiment are very promising from both the technical and business point of view. The number of defects found in the product release has been reduced by 15%. The predictability accuracy has been increased by 10%. The productivity has not been significantly increased however there are strong indications that the long term use of PSP will lead to productivity increase. Furthermore, PSP has been successfully introduced to the Report development process, a non-coding process, which indicates the applicability of PSP to other development processes as well.

The results of the PERSPI project proved that the formal introduction of the PSP in certain processes of the development environment leads in significant benefits. These results justified the continuation of the effort on the personal process improvement within the company's development department. The cyclic enhancement of the PSPs that were designed and introduced in the context of the PERSPI and the introduction of PSP principles in other processes, mainly the Customer Implementation Services and the Technical Support Process, are the next major improvement actions. The PSP introduction has provided the means to target CMM Level 4 in our next major Process Improvement action.

## 10.50   PET 10438

## The Prevention of Errors Through Experience-Driven Test Efforts

Through a rigorous analysis of problem reports from previous projects the companies behind the PET project have achieved a step change in the testing process of embedded real-time software. The measurable objectives have been to reduce the number of bugs reported after release by 50%, and reduce the hours of test effort per bug found by 40%. Both of these goals have been met. The actual numbers achieved were 75% less bugs reported, and a 46% improvement in test efficiency.

The problem reports have been analysed and bugs in them categorised according to Boris Beizer's categorisation scheme. We have found that bugs in embedded real-time software follow the same pattern as other types of software reported by Boris Beizer.

We have also found that the major cause of bugs reported (36%) are directly related to requirements, or can be derived from problems with requirements. Improved tracking of requirements through the development process has been achieved through the introduction of a life-cycle management CASE tool. Unfortunately the customisation of the life-cycle management tool took longer than expected, so no actual numbers on the positive effect of the tool are available at present, but it is expected that the integration and system testing phases can be combined, resulting in a major reduction of testing effort.

The second largest cause of bugs (22%) stems from lack of systematic unit testing, allegedly because of the lack of tools for an embedded environment. We have found that tools do exist to assist this activity, but their application requires some customisation. We have introduced a unit testing environment based on EPROM emulators enabling the use of symbolic debuggers and test coverage tools for systematic unit testing. The unit testing methods employed were: Static and dynamic analysis.

We have demonstrated that the number of bugs that can be found by static and dynamic analysis is quite large, even in code that has been released. The results we have found are applicable to the software community in general, not only to embedded real-time software, because the methods and tools are generally available. Finally a cost/benefit analysis of our results with static and dynamic analysis indicates that there could be an immediate payback on tools and training already on the first project.

The efficiency of static analysis to find bugs was very high (only 1.6 hours/bug). Dynamic analysis was found to be less efficient (9.2 hours/bug), but still represented a significant improvement over finding bugs after release (14 hours/bug). We achieved a test coverage (branch coverage) for all units in the product of 85%, which is considered best-practice for most software, e.g. non safety critical software.

The PET project has been funded by the Commission of the European Communities (CEC) as an Application Experiment under the ESSI programme: European System and Software Initiative.

## 10.51  PIBOP 23825

### Process Improvement Based on PSP

This report describes acquired experiences during the execution of the ESSI Process Improvement Experiment PIBOP (Process Improvement Based on PSP). The objective of the PIBOP experiment was to introduce W.H. Humphrey's Personal Software Process (PSP) approach at Intracom's Software Development Centre (SWDC). PSP, focusing mainly on the individual software developer level, allows for systematic implementation of proven practices on planning, tracking and analysis of software development work and products, while specific measurements are used to support monitoring and evaluation of these practices. PSP besides personal improvement, improves the overall process, achieving better SPI understanding and commitment by all involved personnel.

The initial step of the PIBOP PIE involved the setting-up and integration of the experiment within a typical baseline project. Then, introduction and training on the PSP method was carried out, and the specific adaptation procedures for the baseline project were documented. Finally PSP was executed throughout the baseline project and the PIE results were evaluated based on appropriate measurements.

The co-ordinator (prime user) of this PIE is Intracom which hosts the PIBOP experiment in one of its projects identified as baseline for the PIE. The PIBOP experiment was supported by external services, essentially training.

The transferability of the experience drawn from the PIBOP experiment is supported by the fact that the content of the experiment is of broad interest and of wide applicability, based on an internationally acclaimed method (PSP). Additionally, PSP is well suited to complement and support potential improvements within organisations. The dissemination actions related to PIBOP results specifically addressed internal dissemination (Intracom Group), Greek SMEs involved in software development, and wider dissemination through Intracom's European business partners. As part of this wider dissemination activity, Intracom participated in two appropriate external events recognised as CEU dissemination events.

## 10.52   PRAMIS 10836

### System & Software Project Management and Management Accounting Methodology

This document summarises the lessons learned in the ESSI Application Experiment 10836 PRAMIS which relates to the development and evaluation of a system & software project management and management accounting methodology.

The project set out to evaluate existing practices in the partner companies, LABEIN and CCL, and to identify improvements and associated computer based support tools. The project included a nine month pilot experiment to evaluate the impact of the selected techniques and tools on project performance.

The lessons learned mainly relate to the development and deployment of a Project Management Manual, changing established work practices and the challenges associated with specifying, acquiring and commissioning support tools. The issues of corporate culture which such changes imply are a key aspect of such improvements and will be important factors in the success of similar initiatives throughout the EU.

The lessons in this document should be applicable to all organisations which work with a project orientation, among which we could mention, among others, software and systems development organisations, engineering services, etc.

This project was partially supported by the European Commission through the ESSI programme (project No. 10836).

## 10.53   PRIDE 21167

### A Methodology for Preventing Requirements Issues from Becoming Defects

Through a rigorous analysis of problem reports from previous projects Brüel & Kjær has achieved a major change in the requirements engineering process. We have developed and validated an experience based requirements engineering methodology, which has proven to give quantitative as well as qualitative improvements to our products and business.

Through our analysis of error reports in a previous process improvement experiment aimed at improving the efficiency of our testing process, we have found that requirements related bugs are the major cause of bugs. We also found that the vast majority of these problems (85%) were due to missing or changed requirements; and misunderstood requirements by developers and testers.

In both experiments we have categorised bugs according to a taxonomy described by Boris Beizer. For the current PRIDE experiment, however, we have limited the study to those bugs which can be related to requirements issues. We found that requirements related bugs represented 51% of all the bugs analysed.

Furthermore we have found that requirements issues are not what is expected from the literature. Usability issues dominate (64%). Problems with understanding and co-operating with 3rd party software packages and circumventing their errors are also very frequent (28%). Functionality issues that we (and others) originally thought were the major requirements problems only represent a smaller part (22%). Other issues account for 13%. The sum of these figures adds up to more than 100% because one bug may involve more than one issue.

A closer study of the bugs suggested a number of techniques that could prevent a significant number of requirements related bugs.

Since usability issues dominate, the corner stone of the new requirements engineering methodology was to introduce usability tests on very early prototypes. These were aimed at validating the development team's understanding of common use situations (scenarios) for the new product. Focused readings and specific actions to verify the resulting requirements specification were also introduced.

The validation techniques of the methodology were introduced on a real-life development project. On this project we achieved an almost 3 times increase in developer productivity on the user interface, and usability issues per new screen were reduced by 72%. The total number of error reports was reduced by 27%.

More important, however, the introduction of use situations (scenarios) and usability tests resulted in a totally revised user interface, which is regarded as a major breakthrough in understanding and supporting the users' tasks. And the product was released in time for shipments before the end of the financial year.

## 10.54 PROMASYS 23795

### Introduction of a Software Project Management System

The objective of the Experiment is to introduce, test and refine a Project Management System (Method and Tools) to specifically control software development projects. Trough this experiment, we intend to demonstrate the benefits of having software projects realistically planned, managed and under control.

The experiment has been carried out in the context of the development of a major improvement to our logistic and production management system. This will involve the development of new functionality in the raw materials planning area, and adding capabilities to retrieve real production information from the fabrication plant (The name of the baseline Project is "Electrocincado").

Gonvarri's interest in this PIE lies in the fact that the strategy of the company relies on offering new services to its clients such as: electro galvanized steel, blanking cutting, cutting lines 2000 to process Z materials, etc. with a high level of quality. This strategy implies the optimisation of the logistic function an adequacy in the stock levels, a rationalisation of transport costs and the implementation of long term relationships with the clients. As Gonvarri gets bigger, adding new services, products and relationships with customers, it is necessary to develop and implement new and specialised software in order to meet the new requirements.

The experiment to define the new Software Project Management Method will:

- Define a well structured way of producing software project plans.
- Establish a clear set of commitments between software developers and users.
- Clarify the Tracking of Software Projects

## 10.55   PROMISD 21551

### Process Management For Software Development

The purpose of the PROMISD project was to establish an organisational and management process-support infrastructure for Computer Logic's Object-Oriented development process for Client-Server applications called the OMEGA process. The OMEGA Product Line is strategic to the future success of Computer-Logic. A CMM-based assessment of the OMEGA software process and its support environment of the OMEGA product line development at Computer Logic has initially been conducted which indicated in a CMM level 1 organisation and pointed-out several strengths e.g. motivated team, advanced technology approach and supporting management and weaknesses e.g.:

- Lack of detailed documentation and training on the Omega development cycle
- Lack of formal project management process
- Lack of documented key processes (requirements management, project planning & tracking, software quality assurance & software configuration management), and
- Lack of a process & quality group.

These areas were addressed in the process improvement plan.

The main results from the process improvement efforts in the context of PRO-MISD include:

- Advanced to CMM level 2 with strong traces of level 3
- Improvement towards compliance with the ISO 9000-3 recommendations
- Reduced new team members introduction time by nearly 50% and 50% reduction in senior-management involvement
- Enabled to sustain and scale the significant benefits resulting from investments in S/W engineering
- Enabled and supported business expansion.

## 10.56 PROMISED 24149

### Process Improvement in Intelligent Simulation Environment Development

This final report illustrates the results of ESSI project number 24149, a Process Improvement Experiment (PIE), named PROMISED (Process Improvement in Intelligent Simulation Environment Development). The Project started in March 1997 and had a duration of 26 months.

The goal of the experiment was to demonstrate how the use of an assessment method such as SPICE along with specific tools can be applied to help a small team to improve its software development processes.

Before the beginning of the actual experiment, an external assessment of CSTB 1's current software development process had been made on the basis of the ISO-SPICE model. This assessment revealed the weak points of this process. The goal of the experiment was to improve these weak points, learn about the process improvement approach in the context of small teams and disseminate the results, allowing CSTB (and similar organisations or other small project teams) to reconsider their organisational methods in software production using the ISO-SPICE model.

The major improvement reached by the experiment, as originally planned, was to improve the situation where procedures were purely performed on the basis of individual knowledge. A higher level of maturity has been reached, where processes are described and therefore can be repeated by any new contributor.

The external SPICE evaluation conducted at the end of the experiment has shown that, although the original goal of reaching ISO-SPICE Level 3 ("Well defined") now seems a bit too ambitious, a significant step has been taken in the right direction. Important improvements in the Engineering field have also been reached as a "side-effect", although not originally planned.

The experience has shown that SPICE can be tailored to fit the needs of a small project team. It has also shown that the use of a specific tool should not be, as originally planned, the centrepiece of a process improvement experience; the process of finding adapted tools should rather be part of the process improvement effort itself : the method is more important than the tool.

## 10.57   PROMM 10616

### Software Engineering Project Management and Metrication

#### Project Objectives

To experiment with and evaluate the PRINCE project management methodology and Function Point metrication so as to improve overall software engineering productivity, quality and time-to-market, within the framework of a well-defined and established systems development life cycle.

Three Irish Life European subsidiaries also participated in this project. Irish Life UK actively participated in the experimentation phase. XAAR (France) and David (Norway) have contributed primarily to the dissemination phase.

#### Progress and Results

The Preparation Phase of the project, involving the installation of project management methods and tools and establishing baseline metrics, was completed on schedule in July of 1994. Five business projects were then selected for participation in the Experimental Phase which finished in June of this year.

The primary benefits expected from the Application Experiment were,

- Improved estimates on projects leading to better delivery.
- Increased client participation on SE Projects by adopting PRINCE methodology.
- Improved Project Management, specifically in the areas project planning and control.

Overall the project achieved its objectives. The new methods, procedures and tools were developed and implemented on five experimental projects. The evaluation phase involved detailed analysis of outputs from post partum reviews which included detailed productivity, delivery and quality metrics. Our findings and conclusions overall have been positive. Both productivity and delivery metrics on the experimental projects have shown an improvement against the baseline. The improvement in delivery, both time-to-market and schedule variance, being the more significant.

From a business perspective, the new project management methodology has been effective in addressing the client participation issue. Estimation and risk management techniques have allowed us to enter into more realistic contracts with clients.

Despite some difficulties implementing function point counting, the metrics collected to date have been extremely valuable and have allowed us to focus attention on improvement in other aspects of the application development process.

## 10.58   REPRO 21513

## Reuse Process and Organisation improvement experiment

### The Objective

The objective is to introduce and test out organised reuse, using the method set forth by the ESPRIT project REBOOT (project no: 7808). This will be done by implementing development procedures and roles focusing on reuse and building libraries of reusable components. We will measure an overall process improvement on the basis of reuse assessments in the beginning and at the end of the project. The assessments will be related to the Reuse Maturity Model (RMM).

Organised reuse is expected to improve quality, increase productivity and reduce time-to-market.

REPRO has been executed within the Retail division of Provida ASA. Provida is an independent software house operating in an international market, developing large systems for Retail and Corporate Banking.

In addition to the work done at Provida, work was subcontracted to a) SINTEF a Norwegian research institute, who was a partner in the REBOOT consortium b) Westsoft a Norwegian distributor of the a project repository product named Project Gateway (PG4/PG5) and c) ISI a company which provide services related to the tools Process Engineer and Systems Engineer as well as the method Systems Engineering.

We selected two consecutive development projects within our normal work. With financial aid from the EUROPEAN COMMISSION, DGIII-F3, the ESSI program, experiments were carried out on these development projects: organised reuse were introduced as the technology being used, part of extra costs incurred by the switch in technology being supported and financed by the Commission. This report will elaborate on the experience gained in these experiments.

### General Experience

The general validity of organised reuse appears significant. Some key expectations were met and confirmed. Selecting the proper tools and methods, however, appears to be quite critical: many different tools and methods are available, not all are giving the same effects. In addition, we experienced that it is of high importance not to incorporate to many changes in our organisation at the same time.

Increased productivity and reduced time-to-market. Measurements of this effect are obscured by the fact that the selection of our final repository tool came late in the project. Since an evaluation will include training aspects heavily present in the first cases of use, we more or less have to use intelligent guess than proper metrics. Our expectation is a factor 2 in the development phase and a factor 4 in the maintenance phase.

Improved quality. Quality measurements must be based on maintenance experience over some period of time and the numbers we have collected so far is not reliable.

### Communities of Relevance

We believe that our experience related to organisational issues and project management will be relevant for most organisations. The fact that our whole experiment is based on a method, as set forth by REBOOT, assures that other organisations can at least use the same strategy in addressing what seems to be a common problem.

## 10.59   ROADS 21649

## Reuse Oriented Approach for Domain based Software

This document is addressed to the software engineering community. It proposes a view on the benefits and impact on business development that can be expected through the implementation of state of the art software reuse within a product-line strategy. It is based on experiments of the ROADS project conducted in the Thomson-CSF group, and benefits from the support from the European Software Institute. (The work and its dissemination is partially supported by the European Commission)

Using available best practice in reuse, ROADS implemented and developed software reuse within a business development strategy. This took place through experiments initiated from corporate management initiative and involving four Thomson-CSF Business units.

Two complementary business objectives, that were translated in the corresponding aspects of the software reuse implementation, drove the project and were conducted in 5 successive and iterative increments:

- at Corporate level : to increase the average software reuse rate and to decrease the average cost of the reused lines of code through definition and improvement of standard software reuse engineering practices based on a Product Line approach ,

- at Business Units level : to meet more specific business objectives (cost reduction , time-to-market reduction , improvement of reliability) through this Product Line approach,

This was conducted through a product-line-based strategy and the analysis of commonalties and variations between specifications and products, leading to the evaluation of reuse potential benefits and constraints.

ROADS is a total success in reaching these objectives: the consistent approach in software engineering practice is helping Thomson-CSF keeping software development environment at the leading edge of technology and set up a continuous measurable process improvement based on the SEI reference:

- The total rate of reuse increased from an initial 20% to more than 60%, exceeding the objective of ROADS initially set to 50%.
- A global environment assessing costs and economic relevance has been designed and validated. It showed that for a reuse rate of 50%, the cost of reused software vs. new is in the range of 30%. This decreases to ca. 10% for a reuse rate >90%.
- Business objectives specific to each Thomson-CSF division where met : cost reduction by a factor 2,5 , time-to-market reduced by more than 50%.
- Spontaneous interest from other divisions grew, based upon the visible success and ROADS assets, and led to an implementation of ROADS approach in a series of other Business Units.
- These results have been presented to a series of conferences and workshops related to software reuse, leading to high interest from a variety of global companies.
- Access to reuse strategic issues and technology is available, in complement to Thomson-CSF contacts, from the independent reuse experts at the European Software Institute in Bilbao (Spain).

## 10.60 SELDOM 23838

### An experiment to introduce in a Seltering project Domain Analysis

The objective of SELDOM is to improve the software production process of Thera by the introduction of Domain Analysis method and Design Frameworks. The purpose of these techniques is to provide the basis for a future application of a reuse-centred software development approach.

This process improvement experiment derived from an internal assessment of Thera's software development practices with the goal of facing one of the main identified weakness area, that is represented by the early phases of requirement definition and software analysis.

The experiment is organised in three main phases:

- Training, study and adaptation of a Domain Analysis methodology.
- Application of the Domain Analysis method to a baseline project, performing the following activities: Domain model definition, Design Frameworks definition, Application of domain models and frameworks to the baseline project.
- Data collection, analysis and comparisons of data collected and dissemination of the results. The project has been successfully performed and the three main phases have been accomplished.

The metrics we adopted to evaluate the experiment are based on product measures (in particular reuse indicators and quality indicators), while effort measures were collected along the project through a monitoring program.

After analysing the results of the experiment, we can draw the conclusion that the introduction of Domain Analysis has been positive under both a qualitative and a quantitative point of view. In particular, it allowed to achieve important benefits in front of the main expected objectives:

- better organise the knowledge of the application domain,
- increase the effectiveness of software reusability policies and reuse practices,
- improve the analysis and design of the products,
- improve the quality of the of the software process (and therefore products).

The results of the experiment are interesting for software firms and developers in the European Community, providing them a convincing evidence that Domain Analysis methods and Design Frameworks are worthwhile to adopt.

SELDOM is financially supported by the European Commission as a Process Improvement Experiment (PIE) within the European Systems & Software Initiative (ESSI).

## 10.61   SERAD 10355

### Software Error Administration Using the GNATS System

This report describes the Application Experiment SERAD *Software Error Administration Using the GNATS System*, which has been supported by the European Commission under the ESSI project 10355.

Subject of the experiment was the implementation of a problem report management system into the already existing software development and maintenance environment of the standard application software PERMAS, which is a general-purpose finite-element analysis software.

The report describes the software background and, in particular, the practice of software problem administration before and during the Application Experiment.

The work performed comprises an assessment of current practice and the implementation and use of the problem report management system GNATS. Because this system allows for e-mail-based problem reporting, this makes it best-suited for a distributed multi-user environment.

The growing archive of problem reports allows not only for a statistical evaluation to derive quality metrics for the underlying software but also for significant improvements of the user support and hotline services. Among others, this leads to an increase of productivity of the support activities.

Based on high acceptance by the users and the software engineers as well as positive results with the experiment, INTES and its partners realised an increase of product and service quality related to the application of the problem report management system.

Beside the effects for the partners in the project, the general approach of introducing a problem report management system can be easily adopted by other software developers. So, the experience in this project may be transferable to other software processes.

## 10.62  SIMTEST 10824

### Automated Testing for the Man Machine Interface of a Training Simulator

The project is funded by the EEC in the frame of the ESSI project; the goal of ESSI is to promote improvements in the software development process industry, to achieve greater efficiency, higher quality and greater economy.

This initiative required to select a baseline project (i.e. an existing development activity) upon which a new approach on some part of the life cycle could bring significant results in the above mentioned areas.

Dataspazio has successfully proposed SIMTEST, the evaluation of automated testing (i.e. the testing supported by a software tool) of the real time simulator of the SAX satellite (SAXSIM).

The experiment is meant to evaluate the differences between a "traditional" approach to testing (i.e. manual execution of test procedures coded by the developer) against the automated approach (i.e. automatic execution of test procedures where part of the code is automatically obtained by describing the expected behaviour of the test).

The automation of integration and test has shown important results:

- less expensive testing
- more reliable procedures
- test repeatability.

Mainly, lessons learned that have been derived from this experiment can be so summarized:

- it is better to take into account the use of these tools at a very early stage of system design as they could require architectural and/or implementation peculiarities;
- automatic test procedures can be more exhaustive and can produce a better coverage w.r.t. the traditional approach. This is paid with an extra effort in their preparation, although capture and playback features can ease the MMI test coding. An economical return is mainly possible for systems which undergo many changes during their operational life and for which non-regression testing is a significant cost;
- the quality and the robustness of the software to be produced is better assured, as more deep and intensive tests can be easily implemented and run with a low cost;
- the repeatability of the tests is really granted using an automated tool, as there are no way to misunderstand or not fully perform a test step, as during manual test execution;
- if properly planned, the testing tool can do much more than just test for the system: it can effectively be used to encapsulate the application under development, reproducing the context environment and facilitating the integration.

As a result of the experiment, our Company is carrying out an evaluation of the use of the same approach for a new development in a similar application; the quantitative data collected during the experiment are being the basis for this decision.

## 10.63  SMETOSQA 10218

## Preparing SME Software Houses to SQA Implementation

A was aimed to select, install, and evaluate Software Engineering (SE) practices in a software development process for industrial control systems in a small enterprise (SME). SMETOSQA covered the following areas:

- Requirements management;
- Modelling of the systems development life cycle;
- Co-ordination and communication with non-software groups involved in system design;
- Planning and tracking of the project.

A measurement mechanism was set up to assess the impact of the new practices on productivity and product quality.

SMETOSQA focused on organisation, methodology and supporting technology.

Two partners were involved: the prime user Infogea S.r.l. a SME producing weight control systems, and the prime user's most relevant customer MG2 S.p.A.

a producer of automated dosing machines for the pharmaceutical industry. MG2 has no direct involvement in the production of software but can significantly bene-fit from software process improvement initiative since software is rapidly becom-ing a core component of its product.

Our initial problem can be summarised as follows: we had to *achieve compli-ance with the requirements of ISO 9001* because of the regulations concerning the validation of computerised systems in our main area of activity: process control in the pharmaceutical industry. However, given the initial state of our systems devel-opment process, the practices connected with Software Quality Assurance (SQA) were not immediately applicable. For this reason we applied for an experiment which covered the installation and evaluation of the founding SE practices ena-bling SQA implementation.

Two formal audits to assess compliance to ISO 9001 were performed, one at the beginning and one at the end of the AE.

Third party assistance on SE and software quality was provided to Infogea by GEMINI, a not-for-profit consortium of software producers; further external sup-port was acquired to carry out our internal training programme.

The AE followed a phased workplan which consisted of:

- An initial assessment, followed by the analysis of its findings which produced an improvement plan focused on process and people.
- Definition of a systems development life cycle based on the V-model, key SE practices were selected and applied to fully support the life cycle.
- Training on SE and SE practices.
- Tools selection, customisation and experimentation.
- Definition and implementation of a data collection and analysis process to assess the results achieved by applying the new practices.
- Evaluation of the experimentation and review of the SE practices to achieve better applicability, ending with formalisation of the new practices by docu-mented procedures.
- Design of the global structure of a Quality Management System having SQA at its core.
- Final audit to assess progress in the achievement of ISO 9001.
- Dissemination of the results at European and local events.

Overall our conclusions are:

- The AE has given a fundamental contribution to the definition of our software process and no significant activity related to our process has been left out.
- The V-model, enhanced to better fit our needs, has proved usable and particu-larly adequate to our needs.
- The definition of the process has considerably enhanced our capabilities in project estimation and project management.
- The data collection process is a lasting and successful one and it allows us to analyse in a quantitative way the following aspects: product quality, process ef-

fectiveness, project estimation effectiveness and efficacy in the usage of the resources.

- The final audit confirmed that we advanced considerably toward ISO 90001 compliance, which now can be considered a short term achievement.
- All software engineers involved in this experiment achieved the culture and the understanding necessary to apply the new practices and to continuously pursue improvement.
- The further external dissemination actions that we carried out locally confirmed that our experiment was replicable in many other SMEs.
- The full commitment of our industrial partner remains hard to achieve and some better results on requirements management and inter-group co-ordination could have been expected if MG2 had more actively contributed to this experiment.

This AE should interest to
- those in the software development community who are involved in implementing SQA and Quality Management, with a specific focus on SMEs,
- those who are in the process of choosing SE methods and tools to support their process,
- those who are concerned by the issue of involving and motivating technical people in a process improvement initiative.

## 10.64   SO.C.CO.MA 21269

### Software Change and Configuration Management

The PIE has been focused on the Software Change and the Configuration Management system (SO.C.CO.MA).

Since the improvement of the change management process is considered significant for all data processing centres, SO.C.CO.MA project was felt a mandatory step to achieve that objective. Methods and tools have been fully defined and implemented during the project to carry out the management of application software changes and to allow the centralisation of the management process.

This report begins with a brief description of the company background focusing on goals of the PIE. Then the experiment is described following its evolution steps and giving in detail roles involved, procedural steps and work products, pointing out the tools used during the project (Endevor, JCR, Lotus Notes).

In conclusion, the report describes the results achieved under a qualitative and quantitative point of view, then the main lessons learned: both outline the importance of a Configuration System Management in organisations handling a combination of internally and externally developed software.

Furthermore, the SO.C.CO.MA development process and its application have been contributory to the consolidation of a new and strong quality oriented culture inside the company.

## 10.65  SPIRIT 21799

### Software Process Improvement: Recondition Information Technology

SPIRIT is a subproject of the software process improvement project of Baan Development. Baan's business can be characterized as provider of enterprise resource planning (ERP) software-packages (standard software). These products come under the names TRITON (old) and BAAN (new).

Motivations for SPIRIT were:

- Baan Development was assessed at CMM-level 1 (1994).
- The global release of a complex product requires improved reliability: time & quality.
- Major customers appreciate commitment to Process Improvement.

Approach of SPIRIT was a comparison between

- the old Software Development Process (SDP) as used for the development of the Manufacturing package in the TRITON 3 release, and
- the improved SDP as used for the development of that package for the BAAN V release.

Aims of SPIRIT were:

- Uncontrolled delay:           18 %      to < 5%
- Bad fixes per 100 calls:       4        to 2
- Post-release defects per Kloc:  2        to < 1

The enormous growth of Baan had some impact on SPIRIT: extension of the duration (from 18 till 24 months) appeared necessary due to a rescheduling of the baseline project and the second aim (bad fixes) had to be adapted because of a reorganization of Baan Development. Moreover the approach of SPIRIT required adaptation because insufficient reliable data on TRITON 3 was available.

This document describes the four topics highlighted below:

- *Project goals:* SPIRIT aims to demonstrate that improvement of the Software Development Process (SDP) results in predictable SW-delivery and quality.
- *Work done:* SPIRIT incorporates assessment, development and implementation of software development process (SDP) practices following the CMM approach for development of BAAN V Manufacturing.

- *Results achieved:* SPIRIT reveals that we have currently the capabilities for CMM-level 2 and are approaching CMM-level 3.
- *Significance:* SPIRIT enables organizations to benefit from our key lessons:
  - how to structure an SDP to enable controlled development in parallel with further process improvements,
  - how to make an SDP description accessible to facilitate its application in daily practice,
  - how to measure the kind of objectives as defined for SPIRIT and immediately feedback the measured results to all persons involved so that they are enabled and motivated to adjust timely.

The Commission of the European Community (CEC), funded SPIRIT as a process improvement experiment (PIE), under European Systems and Software Initiative (ESSI) project number 21799.

## 10.66  TPM 21336

## Towards Total Product Management in Tecnopolis

The results of the Total Product Management (TPM) process improvement project should be of interest to managers and R&D personnel. The target audience is especially the in rapidly growing small and medium sized software companies specialising in packaged software products. The objectives of the project were to improve the maturity of the software product management (SPM) processes of the participating three companies. The maturity assessments carried out in the beginning and in the end of the project show that this objective was also reached in the project.

The improvements in the SPM processes of the companies have led to increased efficiency of production, savings of time and improved customer satisfaction. It is very apparent that as a software company grows and the number of customers increases, the SPM processes must improve. If improvement is neglected, the company will lose its competitiveness. The practical level achievements of the companies can be listed as follows:

- reduced time spent for solving product management related problems
- faster response times to customer service requests
- higher customer satisfaction gained by improved product support system
- improved quality of the products
- improved efficiency in the production
- faster building and re-building times of different product versions.

One of the lessons we have learned is that collecting metrics is very demanding, but the results have proven to be very useful in securing management commitment and for convincing the developers of the usefulness of process improvement. We also found that an initial assessment together with final assessment are essential in the process improvement activity. It pinpointed the areas most in need of improvement and finally also the areas where some improvement had taken place. The need for continuous process improvement is also one of the key lessons of this project.

The PIE was divided into five main phases: 1) maturity assessment of the companies in the beginning of the project, 2) definition and implementation of the version control process and tools, 3) definition and implementation of the configuration management process and tools, 4) definition and implementation of the product management process and tools, and 5) maturity assessment of the companies at the end of the project. As a result of the project, product management processes have been specified and implemented in the context of baseline projects. The dissemination activities have been carried out successfully and the results of the PIE have been presented to a wide audience.

## 10.67  VERDEST 21712

### Software Version Control, Documentation and Test Management

#### Project Goals

The objective of PIE is to purchase and implement version control, document management and automated software testing tools to improve and develop software design and development process itself in our company and in our associated partner organisations.

#### Work Performed and Results

Project gained its functional goals at the scheduled time. The expected technical, business, organisational and skill goals were mostly achieved. The actual cost was about 70 % of the estimated total cost.

The experiment project was divided to three phases.

The first phase of the experiment project focused on the analyses and definitions of our traditional and the objective ways to manage the practices and methods. We also defined specifications of the tools to be used. After this we made a choice of the software tools to be used in the experiment project. We installed also the selected tools to our use. The result of the first phase was the summary documentation of defined practices and tools.

The second phase of the experiment project focused on the implementation activities. This included more detailed definitions of the workflow management and how these definitions should be brought into use in the daily operations and routines in the baseline project. This phase included also user training activities. We also got preliminary results of the project concerning testing and version management.

The third and last phase of the experiment project included document management based on Intranet-solution including user training activities. The result measurement as well as the result comparisons to other projects was also included to this project phase.

# Index

Druck:        Strauss Offsetdruck, Mörlenbach
Verarbeitung: Schäffer, Grünstadt